WORSHIPPING ECUMENICALLY

Edited by Per Harling

WORSHIPPING ECUMENICALLY

Orders of Service
from Global Meetings
with Suggestions for Local Use

WCC Publications, Geneva

Second printing August 1998

Cover design: Edwin Hassink
Cover photo: TIB

Hymns edited and typeset by Terry MacArthur

ISBN 2-8254-1141-8

© 1995 WCC Publications, World Council of Churches,
150 route de Ferney, 1211 Geneva 2, Switzerland

Printed in Switzerland

Contents

The Liturgy of the World:
Ecumenical Worship with All Senses
Per Harling

1

1. Worship Services in the Perspective of Mission

27

2. Services Using Water as the Central Image

83

3. Services for Liturgical Seasons

104

4. Services on Justice, Peace
and the Integrity of Creation

116

5. Prayer Services

136

6. Lima Liturgy

155

7. Walking the Way of the Cross

169

Index of Music

180

Sources

182

18.95

(30217

The Liturgy of the World:
Ecumenical Worship with All Senses

Per Harling

It was an early morning in May 1989, and it was already hot although the sun had not yet risen over the Trinity University campus in San Antonio, Texas, USA, the site of a world conference on mission and evangelism organized by the World Council of Churches. As often happens, the worship life, with its multi-cultural, symbolic and musically colourful expressions, had become the very heart of this ecumenical gathering.

For the worship on this particular morning, over 800 people joined in "Walking the Way of the Cross", following Christ's way of suffering, death and resurrection and expressing solidarity with those people around the world who face a difficult and painful walk every day. As the member of the conference worship team with special responsibility for this morning experience, I moved back and forth among the eight stations of the walk to see whether anyone needed assistance. There was one station where I spent more time than at the others. It was called "Meditation on Nailing", and the worship team had some doubts about how people might react to it. Had we gone too far? A huge log was placed on the ground. As people approached it, they heard the sound of hammering; and upon arriving each person was given a nail, a pencil and a piece of paper. They were invited to write personal or communal sins on the paper and to nail it to the "cross", acknowledging that "by his wounds we are healed".

So many things happened to so many people at this station, and I was moved and fascinated. Especially I will never forget the experience of an elderly theologian, who was obviously unaccustomed to using a hammer. He failed several times and wept heavily, but he was determined to get the nail down through his own sheet of paper with its list of sins into the log. And after some time he did succeed in this deeply moving symbolic action.

A few hours later I met him during a coffee break and we began to talk about the early morning walk. He told me that the "Meditation on Nailing" had moved something deep within him. "You know," he said, "I have devoted my whole life to theological study, especially of the role of reconciliation in the life of the church. But today, as an old man, I was — almost for the first time in my life — deeply and personally touched by its overwhelming meaning."

These words of an old theologian say something very important about liturgy: that faith needs not only words to be understood and lived out; it needs all senses, the whole body. A Lutheran bishop once put it this way: "Not even a Lutheran is only a soul with ears!" The understanding of liturgy as something speaking to all the senses is a truth of which the Spirit is reminding the churches today. The longing for more living, valid and true expressions of worship is widespread today because it is more clearly understood that at the heart of the church is the liturgy of the church. What we believe is shown, narrated and lived out through the liturgy. *Lex orandi, lex credendi.*

During the last decades ecumenical worship has undergone amazing developments. A friend wrote to the worship committee after the San Antonio conference: "Something of tremendous significance for the future strengthening of the ecumenical vision may be happening in the amazing revolution in ecumenical worship." Many people have sensed this in their own ecumenical experience. Despite other problems, we have continued to find new ways to sing together, to pray together, to share our pain, our joy and our faith together within old and new liturgical expressions. It is helpful to look briefly at the history that lies behind this development.

THE DEVELOPMENT OF ECUMENICAL WORSHIP

Four important movements

When the church history of the twentieth century is written, four movements will certainly be highlighted: the *ecumenical*, the *missionary*, the *liturgical* and the *charismatic* movements.

These four movements are certainly interrelated; indeed, it was the international mission conference in Edinburgh in 1910 which is often identified as the birth of the ecumenical movement. In the beginning the ecumenical movement engaged white, male clergy from the West, but it soon grew into a global and multi-cultural movement — of which the World Council of Churches, with more than 320 member churches, is an important instrument and in which lay people and women play an important role. Apart from mission, two other streams flowed into the widening ecumenical river: Life and Work and Faith and Order. All these streams have made their input into the liturgical development of ecumenical worship life.

If the ecumenical movement has led to an intensive search of each other's traditions within Christianity, the twentieth century has also been dominated by an outward movement, the globalizing of Christianity. Today more than 60 percent of Christians live in the southern hemisphere, and the churches there are growing, while church membership in the North and West is declining, in some places rapidly. This change in the map of the Christian church has changed the face of the ecumenical movement. A comparison between the first mission conference in 1910 and the most recent in 1989 shows what has happened during this century: in Edinburgh nearly all delegates were Protestant white men of "mature" age from the USA and Europe. In San Antonio 70 percent of the delegates came from Third World countries, 43 percent were women and 15 percent young people. The experience of faith is now more rooted in non-Western cultural, political and social soil; and people in the North and West are increasingly becoming receivers of these experiences of newly formulated theology in art, music and liturgy.

Beginning mainly as a development within the Roman Catholic Church, the liturgical movement grew out of a renewed interest in the medieval heritage. A breakthrough came in 1963 with the Second Vatican Council's Constitution on the Sacred Liturgy (*Sacrosanctum Concilium*), which not only brought the Roman Catholic Church nearer to Protestant liturgical understandings but also influenced liturgical development in most Western Christian traditions. The liturgical movement has underlined, among other things, the communal character of the liturgy, the active participation of the people, the importance of biblical teaching and the adaptation of local cultural traditions and expressions.

The fourth dominant movement in twentieth century church history has many branches, but its roots are in the Pentecostal tradition. The charismatic movement is responsible for much of the mission work in the world today, using strong para-church organizations, modern technology and unconventional methods to reach masses of people. New independent churches and congregations are born every day. At the same time the charismatic movement has made a strong impact within many Protestant and Catholic parishes. Liturgically "free" charismatic expressions have opened up many older traditions to a more spontaneous worship life.

Factors of change

These four movements have given important impulses to liturgical renewal in many churches. But there are other factors as well.

NEW LITURGICAL BOOKS

The past twenty years have seen the development of many new worship books, hymnbooks and Bible translations. Even churches of "non-liturgical" traditions have produced their own worship books. Though from different traditions these new materials display a surprising unity in structure and content and reflect a common view of the form and shape of worship, which is a consequence of the liturgical movement. Nowhere is this uniting power of liturgy more evident than in singing. There are few dogmatic barriers in singing, and new songs are being shared more than ever across denominational lines. For example, the different churches in Sweden all published new hymnbooks in 1986. In each, the first 325 hymns are the same. The fact that we are sharing each other's songs has brought Christians together as never before.

WOMEN'S PERSPECTIVES

The voices of women have become increasingly stronger within all levels of society, including the churches. The Ecumenical Decade of the Churches in Solidarity with Women (1988-1998) is just one sign of this movement.

"Women's theological experiments with their spiritual experience have blown a new wind into the church," writes Suzanne Fageol. "The church, which resides on the plain of certainty, has, in turn, shouted for the breezes to cease. But the Spirit has called us and we cannot be stopped from journeying into a new land."[1] The new theological insights formulated by women theologians have gained attention in liturgy as well. At the same time, more and more denominations are ordaining women, which has naturally influenced the liturgical expressions of those churches.

Women have sharply criticized the exclusiveness of traditional liturgical language, above all, the use of male language for God and for human beings in general ("man" and "mankind" in English). Within liturgical circles there has been considerable discussion of these issues; and Gail Ramshaw-Schmidt points to an "emerging consensus" on principles concerning language for God in the liturgy:

> 1) human language cannot adequately express the divine; 2) yet Christians are required to speak communally; 3) religious language utilizes metaphoric speech; 4) the Judaeo-Christian God has no sexuality; 5) the word "God" in contemporary English is not a gender-specific noun; 6) Jesus is both God and a human male. More and more people are discovering ways to alter their speech and to nuance their writing in adherence to these principles so that their language comes to witness to the paradoxes of Christian speech and of an incarnate God.[2]

Many denominations, especially in the USA, have revised their liturgical books to alter the language along these lines. Although there is no unitary agreement within the ecumenical movement, the WCC seeks in worship at its meetings to use inclusive language as much as possible, at least concerning humanity. In the preparation of worship for the seventh assembly in Canberra (1991), interim guidelines on this issue were formulated:

> a. Reaffirm the trinitarian basis of the WCC and the credal/baptismal formula as biblical language about God. Therefore, do not refrain from reference to the Father, Son and Holy Spirit when appropriate.
> b. Avoid personal pronouns in reference to persons of the Trinity whenever possible.

c. Supplement our customary vocabulary and language by increased use of feminine, especially biblical, imagery.

d. Use of terms such as Creator, Redeemer, Sanctifier is appropriate language for speaking about God, but some traditions do not accept them as direct substitutes for the biblical language referring to the persons of the Trinity.

e. Biblical quotations from standard translations are not to be modified, nor are direct quotations from the creeds, the Lord's prayer and other writings. Where necessary, supplementary comments may be added to make such quotations more inclusive.

But as Rosemary Radford Ruether notes, the contribution of women to liturgical development goes beyond raising the question of language. She speaks of "an increasing recognition that women have been left out of the religious tradition. Their history has not been remembered; their pain and hope have not been lifted up as a content for religious experience and celebration. This impels them to create new symbols and stories to express their experience."[3] Thus new biblical images and stories are employed and new liturgical expressions are developing. Suzanne Fageol says that

> one gift of feminist theology to the church is its insistence that worship and spirituality must be embodied. We have our relationships with God and with others as flesh and blood creatures. For too long, however, the emphasis in patriarchal theology has been on affirming the spirit and denying and denigrating the flesh.[4]

Above all, the feminist liturgical movement has created strong ecumenical networks, not only drawing in a broad spectrum of Catholic and Protestant women, but also reaching out to similar movements among other religions.

GLOBAL REALITY

Throughout the world people are becoming increasingly aware of global realities. Never before have people moved across national borders as much as today, and religious traditions are encountering each other more than ever. A particular reflection of this in ecumenical worship is the influence of the Eastern Orthodox churches on the West. Openness to and interest in Orthodox expressions of faith have led to new liturgical attitudes in Western churches.

Another significant change has come from the migration to the cities. At the beginning of this century only 9 percent of the world population lived in cities; by its end more than 60 percent will. This worldwide movement, the "largest migration in the history of humankind", constitutes a great challenge for Christian mission and worship.

Along with this has come globalization in the field of technology. The communications and information industries have reduced the impact of geographical and cultural distances, offering new possibilities and posing new challenges for liturgists.

LAY PARTICIPATION

Worship, which has long been the responsibility of the clergy, has undergone a tremendous "democratization" in many church traditions. The changes in Roman Catholic worship promulgated by the Second Vatican Council have influenced other traditions to allow lay people take more responsibility in local worship life. Worship is seen as the responsibility of all God's people in each place — a return to the practice of the earliest Christian church. "When you come together, *each one* has a hymn, a lesson, a revelation, a tongue or an interpretation. Let all things be done for building up," Paul writes to his friends in Corinth (1 Cor. 14:26), exhorting them to use everyone's gifts in their common liturgy. Consequently, the pastor is no longer the one who plans and does everything, but now functions more as a worship co-ordinator, with a special role in most traditions for administering the sacraments and teaching.

WORSHIP AND CULTURE

Liturgy has deep roots. The liturgies of some churches preserve patterns from the first centuries of the Christian church. In most Orthodox liturgies very little has changed during the last thousand years. "High-church" traditions still use liturgical vestments introduced into the church during the fourth century and influenced by how people then dressed in Roman court circles. Nevertheless, liturgy has always been shaped by its time and culture. Revival movements, breaking from established church traditions, have often created their own worship expressions out of elements from the contemporary popular culture. Today many churches are opening themselves to the surrounding popular cultures in music, the use of symbols, gestures and language. "The church and the people found a common language when we started to use folk music as an expression of our common faith", a Latin American theologian once remarked to me. But eventually all languages and expressions get old.

CHANGES IN THE WORSHIP PLACE

Developments in the liturgy parallel in many ways the evolution of church architecture. The first Christians met around the meal table in their homes, and it was natural for all to participate. When Christianity became legal and then a state religion in the fourth century, the hidden church came out into the light. Now many people could gather together, and the large halls of the Roman cities, the basilicas, were occupied by Christians. This move radically influenced the shape of the liturgy. Participation was limited. A few persons took over the tasks of many. The liturgy became the domain of the clergy.

In the Western rite during the middle ages the altar, the meal table, was moved far away from the people. For a long period of time there were two rooms in the worship place: one for the clergy (the sanctuary) and one for the people. The liturgy took place behind the demarcation separating the two rooms. The Reformation in the West removed this barrier between the sanctuary and the rest of the church, reopening the way to the altar to the people, but the dominance of the clergy remained.

The history of liturgy in the West might be summarized briefly as follows:

• In the earlier Christian churches worship was something *done* in memory and in praise of the risen Christ.

• During the middle ages worship became something *said* in memory and in praise of the risen Christ.

• During the Protestant Reformation worship became something *heard* (and understood) in memory and in praise of the risen Christ.

The return in many quarters to the liturgy of *doing* requires changes in the place for worship. Many new churches (at least in the West) are now designed with the altar as a focus and the community placed around it in a semicircle. In the altar area other liturgical elements are placed: the baptismal font, musical instruments, the choir. This architecture attempts to make possible participatory liturgy, the liturgy of doing. Such liturgy using all the senses recognizes the wisdom of an old Chinese proverb: What you hear, you will forget; what you see, you will remember; what you do, you will understand.

Worship in the World Council of Churches

Discussion of worship began very early in the life of the World Council of Churches. Already the second meeting of the WCC central committee, in Chichester in 1949, discusssed the possibility of shaping an ecumenical worship order. An ecumenical worship book was suggested, which would contain "a selection of the great common inheritances, e.g., Psalms and other selections from the scriptures, some of the ancient canticles, the Lord's Prayer, etc., a section containing examples of some of the most distinctive treasure of our various traditions" and a section with examples of how to combine the other two sections for special services. A warning was issued against the danger of "Western provincialism" and a recommendation was made "to draw upon the hymnology and devotion of the Eastern church tradition".

The theological discussion of worship was on the agenda of the Faith and Order movement, and in preparation for the third world conference on Faith and Order (Lund 1952), a book on *Ways of Worship* was published[5]. It dealt with such issues as the elements of the liturgy, the meaning behind words and sacraments in the different traditions and "liturgy and devotion". During the conference itself participants discussed eucharist and baptism, lay participation, the difference between liturgical and "non-liturgical" worship expressions and the issue of faith, liturgy and culture.

Throughout the history of the WCC such questions of liturgical theology, function and content have engaged the member churches, both internationally and regionally, with representatives from Third World churches taking an increasingly vocal part in the debate. For example, when the first assembly of the All Africa Conference of Churches (Kampala 1963) struggled with questions of worship, delegates were critical of liturgies imported from the West, which did not care about African spirituality, noting that "their unsuitability is due principally to the fact that they did not grow out of the life of a living church in Africa".[6]

The WCC's fourth assembly (Uppsala 1968) devoted an entire section to "Worship in a Secular Age", and its report issued wide-ranging challenges to the worship life of the WCC member churches: "We are bound to ask the churches whether there should not be changes in language, music, vestments, ceremonies, to make worship more intelligible;... whether lay people should not be encouraged to take a greater share in public worship; whether our forms of worship should not avoid unnecessary repetition, and leave room for silence..."[7]

But practical ecumenical worship life was still in its infancy. Apart from the official opening and closing worships, morning and evening services at Uppsala followed the form of the different traditions, which then invited people to take part in their liturgies: one morning a Lutheran worship, another morning an Orthodox, and so on. This pattern of "confessional" ecumenical worship goes back to the second world conference on Faith and Order (Edinburgh 1937), when "each day began and ended with prayers conducted by delegates... In the mornings each leader 'followed the accustomed use of his own tradition'. It seems that this was the first time that morning prayers were conducted in this manner."[8]

In the WCC's fifth assembly (Nairobi 1975), an assembly worship committee sought to integrate worship life with the rest of the assembly's work. A brief (15-minute) order of worship was prepared which was "suitable for use at a plenary session... It can be used at the beginning or the end of a session, or the moderator may decide at some point during the session to interrupt the business in order to worship God and to ask his help."[9]

This way of worshipping was something new to the ecumenical movement, "a fairly determined break with precedent", as David M. Paton described it in the report from Nairobi. "Worship has often been the weakest part of ecumenical meetings because it is the point at which, sometimes without recognizing it, we are most dependent on familiarity not only of liturgy and language but of style and even intonation."[10] But Paton also noted a serious problem with this new way of doing worship: its effectiveness depended to a great extent "on where you were sitting in a very large hall that did not lend itself to worship". This would lead to an important breakthrough at the next assembly: the use of a special worship tent.

The Nairobi experience was developed further at the world mission conference in Melbourne in 1980. In particular Melbourne highlighted three important liturgical elements: the use of short, sung liturgical acclamations (Kyrie, Hallelujah, Gloria) from different traditions around the world; visualization and unconventional use of symbols and symbolic actions; and participation of many people, lay and ordained, in the liturgical action.

The WCC's sixth assembly (Vancouver 1983) has often been referred to as the "worshipping assembly". In addition to the large opening and closing worships and the celebration of the Lima liturgy — an ecumenical eucharist developed to express the convergence reflected in the 1982 Lima text on *Baptism, Eucharist and Ministry* — worship was celebrated each morning in a large worship tent. In the delegates' official evaluation of the assembly, more than 90 percent mentioned worship as its most significant aspect.

What gave the worship in Vancouver such a great impact? I would suggest ten factors, which I believe have wider implications for any reflection on what makes ecumenical liturgy come alive:

1. The services were very carefully planned and tested. All worship texts and music were checked to ensure cultural diversity and sensitivity to confessional and language issues. The attention paid to detail was rewarded in services that proceeded smoothly, without distraction.

2. In planning the assembly's worship life, the group responsible worked carefully to avoid the often Protestant temptation of taking an instrumental view of worship, which had been common at earlier ecumenical meetings. In Vancouver God was worshipped; the services were not used for other purposes (making a point, highlighting an "issue").

3. The order of worship used each morning followed a simple form built up out of elements from the earliest Christian worship traditions and thus accepted by most traditions.

4. The use of a tent as the place of worship was important for several reasons:
— The tent was a confessionally neutral place, arranged explicitly for *ecumenical* worship.
— Using the tent avoided the difficulty of worshipping in the plenary hall, which was a basketball gymnasium.
— Biblically and liturgically a tent evokes the "pilgrim people" (who worshipped in a tabernacle in the wilderness) and the incarnation of the Word who "became flesh and tabernacled among us" (John 1:14).
— The tent was literally open (one long side of it was open all the time) and inviting in its character.
— The tent provided ample seating (3500), and all worshippers were able to participate on equal terms. No seats were reserved.

5. Music contributed a great deal. Songs, collected from many cultures, were usually sung in the original language. Here the multi-cultural team of skilful animators (cantors) were decisive for involving worshippers by teaching new songs.

6. Many people took leadership roles: during the two-and-a-half-week assembly more than 650 men, women, youth and children, lay and ordained, had some liturgical responsibility.

7. The daily order of worship offered a good balance between solid liturgical structure and a freedom for improvization.

8. Symbols and symbolic actions (many of them participatory) were central. This was important because the tent offered no possibility for simultaneous interpretation. Instead, the symbolic actions were developed as ways of meditating on the word.

9. Many languages were used in the Bible readings. In all, more than forty languages were used during the assembly.

10. The worship book was beautiful and attractive.

The model of ecumenical worship followed in Vancouver has subsequently been used at other large ecumenical meetings. Again at the seventh assembly (Canberra 1991) a worship tent brought more and more people together each morning; and again people talked about the great experience of true ecumenical worship life. The consequences of these experiences have gone far beyond the conferences themselves. "People became aware that there are other languages, other cultures, other resources, other forms of music that are not European or North American. They became aware that there are many places in the world where the expression of faith takes place in different forms, places where the culture is very different from the 'mother culture' brought by their own religious traditions."[11] This new ecumenical worship experience within the WCC has above all helped to bring a new sense of self-respect to Christians from the churches of the southern hemisphere.

But any overview of the history of worship in the ecumenical movement must acknowledge the issue that has proved most difficult of all: eucharistic participation. This division at the Lord's table is often described as *the* scandal of the ecumenical movement. At the local level significant advances have been made in the mutual sharing of the bread and wine among many Western churches. Within the Orthodox families there have been recent steps which will make possible sharing at the Lord's table by Eastern Orthodox and Oriental Orthodox. But it is still impossible for Protestants, Roman Catholics and Orthodox to join in an officially sanctioned eucharist. During the Canberra assembly in 1991 the then WCC general secretary Emilio Castro exclaimed: "Let this be the last assembly at which we have divided eucharist!"

Some features of ecumenical worship

Daily worship at ecumenical conferences has evolved some important typical features, most derived from one or another liturgical tradition, but some developed out of the specific experience of worship in a multi-lingual and multi-cultural context.

THE WORSHIP ORDER

Orders for daily worship may differ slightly from day to day and from conference to conference, but on the whole the same basic pattern — a classical form rooted in the oldest traditions of liturgy — is followed. Usually these are printed and shared before the worship. For example, the daily order used in Canberra had the following general form:

> Preparation (*learning and practice of songs*)
> Invocation or call to worship (*often in a responsive form*)
> Hymn of praise
> Confession of sins, followed by word of forgiveness
> Entry of the Word (*procession and singing*)
> Old Testament or Epistle reading
> Sung acclamation
> Gospel reading

Sung acclamation
Response to the Word (*often some kind of symbolic action*)
Affirmation of faith
Intercessions (*with sung acclamations between petitions*)
Lord's Prayer (*each person in his or her own language*)
Benediction
Hymn

SYMBOLS AND SYMBOLIC ACTIONS

The liturgy of the church has always been rich in the use of symbols and symbolic actions, which can be a more powerful and effective way to communicate patterns of interpretation than words. The word "symbol" is derived from the Greek verb *symballein*, which means "to throw together, to join". In liturgy, therefore, symbols combine the eternal and the temporal, the unspeakable and the speakable. The sacraments are actions in which the presence of the invisible God is made visible. In most traditions the liturgical use of the eucharistic bread and the baptismal water makes them elements of God's presence. At the same time they are strong symbols for the survival of humankind in an exposed world. The cross, the altar, the baptismal font, the features of church architecture are all symbols of something important beyond their material shape. In the same way liturgical gestures are meant to point beyond themselves to the reality and the presence of God.

In international ecumenical worship the main impetus for using symbols and symbolic actions is the difficulty of simultaneous interpretation in a worship service with people of many languages. Consequently, traditional preaching has been reduced in favour of reflection on the Word through the use of symbols and symbolic actions. This does not mean that the ecumenical movement has discarded the important role of the sermon, but the means by which the gospel is proclaimed has changed. Services in Canberra, for example, used candles, icons, eucalyptus trees, fruits, rubbish, water, a globe, chains, ashes, sack cloths, crosses, smoke, incense, photographs and pictures, bread and wine. People were also involved in participatory actions: embracing, holding hands, clapping, shaking hands, dancing and bowing or kissing to greet each other. At every worship the Bible and candles were brought in procession.

MUSIC

Central to the development of ecumenical worship have been changes in music, of which four features may be highlighted:

1. Music in a multi-cultural and a multi-lingual way

Only during the last three decades has indigenous music become widely accepted in the churches of Africa, Asia and Latin America, replacing the exclusive use of European hymns with the words translated into local languages. Instead of considering music as an obvious area in which Christian faith can and should be incarnated within a particular culture, the missionary tradition took European hymns to be the only valid musical vehicle for the gospel. Today, that has changed. New contextual music is being composed as never before in all parts of the world; and through the ecumenical use of this music, it has been shared with other traditions.

For a long time traditional Protestant hymn-singing — a rich heritage of the Reformation — predominated in the ecumenical movement. There seemed to be hesitation about introducing music from Orthodox or Third World traditions. The striking evolution of ecumenical singing is seen clearly in the composition of ecumenical songbooks over the years. The 1957 version of *Cantate Domino* included six songs from Asia and four Orthodox liturgical acclamations out of 120 songs and hymns; the 1974 edition had 38 songs (19 percent) from the South and 13 items (6.5 percent) of Orthodox origin; in the Vancouver worship book (1983) there were 29 songs (48 percent) from Latin America, Africa, the Caribbean and Asia, and the Orthodox input had increased to 14.5 percent; in the Canberra worship book (1991) there were 37 songs (53 percent) of Third World origin.

In international ecumenical worship, songs are usually sung in their original language, for the most important aspect of a culture is its language. For people whose mother-tongue is English and who are used to hearing their own language most of the time in ecumenical meetings, singing during ecumenical worship may be one of the few occasions on which they get a hint of the emotional and intellectual struggle that people from other cultures must go through to listen and to speak at such meetings.

2. The use of short liturgical acclamations in addition to traditional hymn singing

We mentioned earlier the increasing use of acclamations such as Kyrie, Gloria, Sanctus, Hallelujah, Amen and other short prayer acclamations. In the 1957 *Cantate Domino* only the four Orthodox items were of that kind; in the 1974 version there were 37. Half of the songs in the Vancouver worship book were liturgical acclamations and in the Canberra worship book more than 40 out of 70. Three factors may help explain this shift:

— The growing influence of the Orthodox tradition in ecumenical worship. Hymn-singing is a very Protestant phenomenon. In Orthodox worship virtually the whole of the service, except the sermon, is sung or chanted.
— There has been a shift from a sermon-focused worship to a more liturgical and participatory worship structure.
— Teaching new music is easier with short musical phrases, especially in foreign languages.

3. A wider use of different instruments

The shift away from an exclusively Western Protestant hymn-singing tradition has naturally influenced the instrumentation. The organ, so dominant in most European church traditions, may still be used for classical Western hymns, but African drums, Latin American rhythm instruments, flutes, Asian bells, guitars and other stringed instruments are more and more making their way into the ecumenical music experience. And much more singing is a cappella, without any instruments at all.

4. The role of the animators

Music is something we do together, but we often need someone to make music come alive in us. In the development of ecumenical worship, animators (*animateurs*) have played that important role. In Canberra there was a team of seven such persons from the different parts of the world. With the help of a well-rehearsed and enthusiastic conference choir and a team of musicians they made people sing and sometimes even move to the music. Besides being an instructor, the animator should inspire the singing by being a *mirror* to the congregation. The shared joy of communal singing is as much an experience that comes through the eyes as through the engagement of the voice.

Developing patterns in ecumenical worship: a summary

A helpful summary of developments in worship within the ecumenical movement is made by Tom Best and Janet Crawford in an article in *The Ecumenical Review*:

1. Worship is an essential part of the ecumenical vocation. It nourishes the search both for unity and for common witness and service. The worship life of ecumenical meetings is at least as important as its plenary presentations, group meetings and reports.

2. There has been a shift within the ecumenical movement over the years from the common *study* of worship as practised by different traditions to the common *experience* of worship as practised within an ecumenical setting.

3. There has been a growing appreciation that many different confessions share certain patterns of worship. Examples are the service of the word with its structure of hymns, confession, biblical readings and prayers; some evening or compline services; and the basic pattern of eucharistic worship shared by Anglicans, Lutherans and Roman Catholics and others.

4. From the beginning, some worship in ecumenical settings has combined liturgical features from different traditions. Worship in ecumenical settings at the global level has always been multi-lingual and multi-confessional.

5. The variety of *confessional material* in worship in ecumenical settings has increased greatly over the years, as the number and variety of Christian traditions active in the ecumenical movement has increased.

6. The variety of *verbal and musical styles* has also increased greatly. This reflects the growing participation of Christians from all over the world, and an increased respect for the manifold indigenous cultural expressions of the faith.

7. There is a greater appreciation and use of non-verbal elements such as music, symbols and movement within worship, a greater awareness of the creative role of silence within worship and a renewed interest in the active participation of lay people in worship.

8. There is a continuing interest in and evident need for an element of "confessional" worship in ecumenical settings. For some this remains a valuable way of experiencing and understanding Christian confessions other than their own.

9. The question of common participation in the table of the Lord remains complex and difficult. But no question is more urgent for the ecumenical movement as a whole.

10. The widespread (and largely unexpected) use of the Lima liturgy indicates *a need for doctrinal convergences to be embodied in the worship life of the churches and of the ecumenical movement*. This could be a powerful part of the reception process for theological agreements and other ecumenical achievements. This suggests that there should be a closer relationship between ecumenical theologians and liturgists.[12]

About this material

Especially through participants in global ecumenical meetings, ecumenical worship material has been widely disseminated to local communities around the world, probably more widely than any other material from the ecumenical movement. One of the recommendations from the WCC's Canberra assembly, speaking of the central role of worship in the Christian life, noted that

worship in its richness has a variety of dimensions and implications: it relates to evangelism, spirituality, social justice, human values, integrity of creation, unity and peace, even as it celebrates salvation. This concern for the centrality of worship should therefore be further developed within the World Council of Churches. The sharing of liturgical material, music, prayers and forms of worship should be developed as a means of helping local congregations to renewal and participation in the spiritual life of the oikoumene. A new ecumenical hymnbook, including prayers and liturgies, is called for.[13]

This book seeks to answer that recommendation. Compiled here are some of the best ecumenical worships from various conferences and major meetings within the WCC during the last several years.

These liturgies were originally prepared for international ecumenical gatherings in a specific setting and at a particular time. Those who use them in a local congregation or ecumenical setting will want to consider making changes or adaptations according to the circumstances and available resources. In addition, this section is prefaced with some general comments about preparing and conducting ecumenical worship.

Global church music

Few can doubt that music has a powerful influence on our societies today. As Ivor Jones has written,

> Music is universal, a basic and fundamental element in human existence, like a deep shaft sunk into our being. But its universalism is bafflingly complex. The plurality of cultures, the polarity of cultures and dimensions of modern music ensure this... Folk traditions across the world have had hurriedly to be transcribed and recorded, as "the world beat" draws the local and national patterns of melody and rhythm into its remorseless sway. [14]

Music is an international language. Through it we may sense each other's cultures and even come to understand something of the circumstances in which different music is created. The music and songs of the people have played an important social, religious and even political role in every society. A story from South Africa, where this dimension of music has deep roots, illustrates this:

> Above all the South African song is a victory-song, a defiant hymn... Two thousand women and children gathered on a sandy field outside Cape Town. They refused to be separated from their menfolk and be sent to Transkei, a "homeland" a thousand miles away, where starvation and sickness awaited them, a reserve that many never had been in, but which according to the apartheid policy was the only legal domicile for these women. Despite constant harassment from the police, despite the cold and the rain the women stood there round the fires and the wooden cross — and sang hymns.
> After six weeks of unbroken singing the patience of the police ended. Early one morning, just before dawn, they struck. Heavily armed and with dogs they occupied the small hills around the camp. The women gathered round the cross, fell to their knees in the wet sand and prayed. Then they started dancing round the cross, this symbol of folly. The women had lost everything — their homes, their families, their jobs and their possessions. They had nothing more to lose, but everything to win. Therefore they were filled with songs of praise... The police did not dance, and why should they? They had everything to lose and nothing to win... When the sun slowly rose over the mountain peaks, one of the women began with the song "Akanamandla", and in triumph the crowd made for the police-trucks to let themselves get arrested, continuously singing "Akanamandla — He has no power! Hallelujah! Satan is powerless!" [15]

There is power in music. Songs may not change the world, but they will never cease to be instruments of hope in hopeless situations, of power in powerless lives, of praise to the incarnated God.

In 1966, the WCC published *New Hymns for a New Day*. In the introduction some important statements were made and questions posed by Albert van den Heuvel:

> — It is the hymns, repeated over and over again, which form the container of much of our faith. They are probably, in our age, the only confessional documents we learn by heart... Tell me what you sing, and I'll tell you who you are!

— That means, it seems to me, that we can talk about new theological insights as much as we like, but as long as these insights are not translated into liturgical hymns, they will never reach the people... Where are the hymns which speak about the humanization of the structures of our society? Where are the hymns which show our fascination with the humanness of Christ? Where are the hymns which express hope, not in heaven, but on earth...?

— We hear how the world sings. Wherever something happens, people start to sing. In the racial conflict, in the struggle for independence of the southern hemisphere, songs flourish... What the world sings is all right, and many Christians have only learned to sing there...

— I would have thought that the Christian community could only learn to sing again if we were to find the *kairos* of our history, the pregnancy of the times in which we live. One can only sing in the church when one is really connected with the dynamic principle of history...

— New hymns are as important as old ones. And the old ones have to be continually tested, theologically, musically and poetically. Unauthentic language or simply bad music corrupt our faith. They give both the outsider and participant the wrong concept of God. It is not for nothing that the eschatological visions of both Israel and the *ecclesia* include the hope of a new song![16]

Important as these points are, they still reflect very much a Western perspective; and the collection they introduced included only five songs out of 44 from the southern hemisphere. In the mid-1960s the creation of new songs in the churches of the South was in its initial stage. Early Christian missionaries from the West had not only brought along liturgies and songs from their homes to introduce to the newly converted Christians, but they also discouraged the use of traditional musical expressions, lest it remind them of their old faith.

Cult and culture were closely identified, the product of a Eurocentric vision of the world in which Christianity was seen to be such an integral part of European culture that it would not be separated from it... Mission therefore was essentially paternalistic adaptation, the adaptation of European cultural Christianity to the people being evangelized.[17]

After the second world war, however, this attitude slowly changed. In Africa, it was mainly Catholic and Anglican missionaries who started a process of encouraging church music in African style. *Missa Luba*, one of the oldest and best-known examples, comes from the 1950s. It inspired not only African composers, but also Latin Americans and Asians. Christians all over the South became aware that Christian faith and spirituality must take root in each culture. "When I am travelling in the West and have been worshipping in English or some other language for a long time, I get restless", wrote the Sri Lankan theologian D.T. Niles. "I have to go out into the woods somewhere and sing some Tamil lyrics before I find my spiritual balance again."[18]

This process of understanding and exploring Christian faith within each culture has been called contextualization, indigenization, localization and inculturation, though each of these terms is used in different ways and none adequately expresses the process. I-to Loh, professor of church music and ethnomusicology at the Asian Institute for Liturgy and Music in Manila and Tainan Theological Seminary in Taiwan, a frequent consultant to the WCC on music and worship, offers his view on the contextualization of church music, specifically in Asia:

1. Contextualization is *not revivalism*. This movement does not try to bring us back to the old traditions which are thousands of years old and which many today might despise or would like to be free from. By contextualization, we are not attempting to force others to

appreciate or accept the old traditions per se. On the other hand, we are emphasizing the contemporaneity, or better utilizing the elements of modern native culture which are relevant to our time, our place and our peoples so that new messages in the text and music can be communicated more effectively.

2. Contextualization is *not exclusivism*. It does not denounce all theological thoughts, expressions of faith, music, worship and liturgical forms of non-Asian countries. It is rather an effort to widen Asian views and expand Asian knowledge and interest so that Asians can be more objective in appreciating and accepting all manners of Christian expression.

3. Contextualization is *not self expressionism*, a flaunting of one's "exotic" skills. It is, on the contrary, a rediscovery of the essence and values of one's own culture, a cultivation of self-esteem, a search for truth, goodness and beauty in the Christian arts. It is also an affirmation that God is not partial to a particular (especially Western) art form and its Christian expressions, but that all sincere expressions of art are acceptable and pleasing to God. Like the old seed, sprouted by Asian waters, deeply rooted in native soil, bears sweeter fruits, the gift of faith nurtured in sympathetic surroundings leads to a new maturity.

4. Contextualization is, above all, the manifestation of the image of God in humankind. It is the revelation of the mystery of God's creative power as shown in his creation, including human minds that formulate various art forms. And it is our participation in God's continuous creation, letting God transform our culture and arts into dynamic media that will effectively communicate and express the meanings of the gospel to our people today. [19]

The differing moods of Asian songs, the improvized and joyful singing in parts of songs from Africa, the complex rhythms of Latin American and Caribbean songs and the beautiful heritage of Orthodox church music have deepened and broadened the ecumenical worship experience in an extraordinary way. Cultural differences mean that it is not always easy to make all these songs our own — one's ears need to be "retuned" or "born again", I-to Loh suggests — but some knowledge of their background and styles of performance might deepen our sensitivity to them.

ASIAN MUSIC (written by I-to Loh)

Christians in most Asian countries are a small minority. Most Protestant churches in Asia still use Western music in their worship services, but there is a growing understanding of the need to implant the Christian faith into the soil of the different Asian cultures. The Asian Institute for Liturgy and Music seeks to encourage this through educating church musicians, conducting research and publishing resources for the churches in Asia. An important step forward was the publication in 1990 of a new Christian Conference of Asia hymnal, *Sound the Bamboo*. [20]

Asian music treasures diversified tone colours, melodic shapes, subtle ornaments and rhythmic force. Harmony as understood in Western music is almost totally absent. Recent compositions from Asia, however, may show certain affinities to Western music. Although one can hear melodies composed in a diatonic scale (*do re mi fa sol la si do*), with certain cadences similar to major and minor modes, they may show quite different characters. Scales such as "*mi fa sol si do*" and "*do re mi sol la*" are popular in Indonesia and Thailand respectively, but again some of the tones may sound "out of tune" to the Western ear.

Traditional Asian melodies use intervals of various sizes larger or smaller than major or minor seconds or thirds, and they may add many grace notes, using intervals smaller than a minor second, gliding up or down, ornamental attacks or terminal glides at the cadence. Since most of these pitches cannot be reproduced in "well-tempered" Western scales, keyboard instruments cannot do justice to these melodies. Thus bowed lutes (like violins without any frets) or differently tuned flutes are best for playing Asian music.

Drums, especially those which can produce variable pitches and tone colours, such as the Indian *tabla*, and a pair of concussion bells, such as the Thai *ching*, may also enhance the beauty of Asian songs.

AFRICAN MUSIC

Archbishop Desmond Tutu has spoken of the indispensable role played by music and dancing in the struggle for justice, peace and reconciliation in South Africa. "When you participate in a political meeting or the funeral of some hero or heroine of the struggle, the inciting songs make the heart beat even harder and pump the adrenaline into our bodies... Then you realize how exciting it is to live in and be part of this huge movement of liberation."[21]

Tom Colvin, a British United Reformed minister who served for many years as a missionary in Ghana and Malawi, summarizes the style of African singing:

> The sharing of the hymn between leader and people, or the passing of the melody back and forth between two groups of singers, introduces an element of drama and a greater excitement into the church's praise. The repetitive character of the melodies and the habit these hymns have of expanding to a climax elicit a more spontaneous response from and a fuller participation by the worshippers. The customary overlap between verses, and between leader and people, contributes to this cumulative effect. Common in the African church also are the spontaneous improvisation of harmonies (say in thirds or fifths, with treble and bass voices often richly doubling at the octave) and the use of percussion instruments for accompaniment.
>
> Those who sing these hymns are encouraged to interpret them in their own way, in the overlap of voices, the addition of harmonies and the use of percussion and rhythms... In a sense the hymns have been "frozen" by being put on paper. It is up to the singers to "thaw them out" in the singing, and so make them their own. Some of them are alive only when they are danced to because they started life as dance tunes.[22]

In African singing what is important is the function rather than the form of the song. One might even say that it is impossible to sing "wrong". The essential thing is not how you sing, but that you participate with your musical gifts, however limited, and that you mean what you sing and sing what you mean. African songs are collective by nature. Often the boundaries between choir and listeners and choir and conductor shift and may even vanish. African music is, above all, corporal. "It is impossible to sing a hymn without the whole body taking part in the words of praise, just as it is impossible to sing a freedom song without feeling the pain of the whole struggle."[23]

LATIN AMERICAN AND CARIBBEAN MUSIC

Pablo Sosa, an Argentine Methodist pastor, musician, composer and theological teacher, has been a prominent figure in the renewal of Protestant church music in Latin America. In an interview he has summarized some of the important developments in Latin American church music.

> The process of bringing popular and indigenous rhythms into the churches started at the end of the 1950s. The Catholic African mass *Missa Luba* — although it was in Latin — paved the way. It showed that the folk rhythms could be used in the liturgy. *Missa Criolla* was thus composed in Argentina, using the folk rhythms of our country. But even before that I had written my first song in popular folk rhythms. *El cielo canta alegría*, "Heaven is singing for joy", was written in 1958 in the style of a *carnavalito*, one of the most popular and oldest rhythms of Argentina. But I never intended it to be sung in church. I wrote it for a picnic with my theological students. I did not think it was suitable for the church. How wrong I was!

After the WCC assembly in Vancouver in 1983, where we were pushed to sing in many original languages, churches in Argentina realized that we had never sung in the language of our own indigenous people, the Indians. The use of Spanish in our worship services marginalizes many people. Indigenous elements play an important role in all Latin American folk music; and in the creative process of using the rhythms, melodies and languages of indigenous peoples the church slowly begins to open itself to the marginalized in our society. This is the kind of music that people really feel belongs to them. One problem in Latin America is that many people cannot read well, so we need simple texts that can be repeated and thus quickly memorized.

In Latin America and the Caribbean a wide range of rhythms and styles is used; and many sorts of rhythm instruments can accompany singing: congas, claves, bongos and maracas, but also guitars and other similar string instruments, marimbas and the like.

ORTHODOX MUSIC

In most Orthodox churches prayers and songs are chanted or sung unaccompanied. Some of the melodies are so ancient that their origin is lost. The human voice is seen as offering the highest expression of praise to God. However, there is a great variety of musical styles among the Orthodox churches. Church music from the Middle East or Greece is often highly ornamented. The melody is sung in unison with the basses singing a drone on a single pitch. Much of the music is sung by soloists or the choir. In Russia and Eastern Europe choral harmony is much more prevalent, and some of the great composers have written music for the divine liturgy. Often there is a back-and-forth nature to the liturgy between the priests and the choir. These short responses, which can also be sung by the congregation, have become influential in ecumenical worship. In Orthodoxy music is used as the vehicle for prayer and proclamation, not just a warm-up for the sermon, as often happens in Protestant services. Orthodox music also brings with it the sense of rootedness in the long history of the church. This is music that has endured persecution and hardship along with the people who have been nourished by the prayer that it effects.

Global worship in a local context

The world is getting smaller. Cultures and traditions meet as never before. In some areas one may even speak of a "global culture" — for instance, among youth. The motto of MTV, the Music Television channel seen in many countries around the world, seems increasingly true: "One planet, one music!" A "global hit" today is literally a *global* hit. Ivor Jones points out that "significant musical decisions are taken, which cannot always be critically monitored and still less socially controlled, by disc jockeys, recording companies and distributing and advertising agencies, which shape the lives, expectations, language, conversation, standards and tolerance levels of the younger generation". That, he says "is one of the most dramatic events of this century, and it is seldom addressed as the significant issue which it most certainly is". [24]

Large cities around the world struggle with more or less the same problems. Advanced computer systems and other developments in the technology of communication make the local context more and more global. Discoveries in the natural sciences create new problems as they solve old ones. As Bishop Anastasios said at the WCC world mission conference in San Antonio:

Contemporary agnosticism is eating away at the thought and behaviour of city-dwellers. The passage from the "written" to the "electronic" word is opening up undreamed-of possibilities for the amassing of a whole universe of increased knowledge and creating a new human thinking. A new world is emerging. A new sort of human being is being formed. The church, the mystical body of "the one who is and was and is to come", has a pledge and a duty to the march of humanity in the future, the whole society in which it exists as "leaven", "sign" and "sacrament" of the kingdom that has come and is coming. What the church has, it has to radiate and offer for the sake of the world.[25]

This new world situation is the background against which changes in worship are taking place in many liturgical traditions. We have already looked at some factors behind these changes; here we will concentrate on how global ecumenical worship experiences can be implanted in the soil of a local context.

In many places denominational barriers are being torn down and new ecumenical communities are coming into existence. More and more people are coming to see their Christian identity as prior to their denominational identity. In liturgical participation and sharing, these new generations of Christians find a common way of praising God. Some new communities have found ways of doing liturgy that has had a great impact on many people; the well-known examples in Europe are Taizé in France and Iona in Scotland. Their view and practice of worship have had an impact on ecumenical worship in wider circles. The Iona Community's declaration on worship in their local context offers a holistic summary of what many Christians long for in their local worship life in today's world. It is worth quoting at length:

> In worship, the deepest longings of our spirits are expressed — the longing for meaning and purpose, for acceptance and freedom, for celebration and hope. The rituals, signs and symbols of worship help us express this need... [Our] worship attempts to be:

> *1. Incarnational*
> At the centre is the belief that God in Jesus Christ became a human being, like us, and shared fully in all the joys and sorrows, hopes and fears of our lives, to let us know that God loves us, forgives us and wants to give us life in all its fullness. Therefore, there is no part of life that is not within the reach of our faith. The word of Jesus is as much for our work as for our worship, applies as much to our politics as it does to our prayers. We cannot just be "Sunday" Christians, nor can Christianity be just a matter of saving our souls while the rest of the world bleeds to death. Christian faith is about everything in life, small as well as great, ordinary as well as special.

> *2. Historical*
> It draws on the wisdom and experience of the church of our mothers and fathers in the faith. The Celtic church of Columba had a deep sense of the incarnation, and of the glory of God in creation. So we use Celtic prayers of welcome, for work, and in expressing the need of the world. Our worship is historical also in using orders and liturgies which have come down through the ages, like in our Sunday morning communion. These are, if you like, the Shakespeare versions of the salvation drama which put us in touch with our Catholic and Protestant history. They also remind us that we are part of the worldwide church, and that our worship must therefore be:

> *3. Ecumenical*
> We are a community representing many different Christian traditions, and we draw on the richness of these at various times in worship. We share the silent worship of the Quakers, the hymn singing and preaching of the Free churches, the various celebrations of the Christian year from Anglicanism and Roman Catholicism. Our communion is open to all denominations, and we seek to learn from all. We also seek to include all, and so our worship must be:

4. Inclusive

We want all to feel welcome and included, as we believe Christ welcomes all who come, and so we seek to use language and forms which do not exclude anyone's experience by being sexist, racist, too culturally exclusive or only understandable by people who have a university degree or those who have always belonged to the church and understand its language. Therefore, we try to explain in worship why we do things, to teach unfamiliar songs etc., and to work at being fully inclusive of all.

5. Changing

Christian faith changes people. And so, although our worship has deep roots, we also want it to be a spreading tree, seeking to find appropriate ways for modern Christians to express their faith in worship, and to find new ways to touch the hearts of all. Therefore, we are sometimes innovative in worship, and try to be open to new ideas, material and challenges. [26]

THE PROCESS OF INTERNALIZATION

Worshipping is a practice of sharing each other's stories and insights. We are sharing the story of God, which we try to relate to each other's stories in order to understand the complexity of life in the light of God's mercy. When the life of Christ is incarnated in our own life, in our own time and space, we can recognize him and the patterns of God in other human beings and in the course of present events. That is the benefit of liturgical material from all parts of the world: it gives us pictures and insights that deepen our understanding of the world in which Christ is incarnated today. Global ecumenical worship resources can be used both in exploring ways of doing local ecumenical worship and in developing denominational worship itself. With a positive attitude towards other worship traditions, Christians may become more aware of the body of Christ as something built up by many cultures, traditions and languages. Such a process of internalization always needs time. There are some important key words related to this internalizing process:

Understanding and accepting

Christian faith has many expressions. No expression is superior to another, although we are of course more familiar with our own tradition than with others. Faith is not linked to any specific culture or tradition, nor is any one culture superior to another. Faith has always taken root in all kinds of cultural soil. Time and space affect the expressions of faith. As we try to understand other expressions of faith, our own faith can deepen and mature; and in that maturing process we may be able to experience other ways of worshipping. In many local settings people have thus realized that liturgy unites. The work for unity always begins with an attitude of understanding and acceptance.

Learning

To do is to learn. Communal learning to use new expressions of faith — such as symbols and symbolic actions — always requires perseverance and good leadership so that people feel secure in their participation. A process of learning takes time. But it is actually only by doing that one can fully understand and maybe even embrace something new.

Acknowledging and affirming

"We have realized that our way of doing worship is not the only one, and that our worship is even incomplete without the others," a local pastor once said after introducing global worship resources in his own congregation. His words mirrored the community's acknowledgment and affirmation of the enrichment they had received through their openness to other traditions.

LEARNING MUSIC

We have mentioned several times the important role played in the development of global ecumenical worship by the use of songs from all parts of the world. The songs suggested for the liturgical material in this book are of course only options, which can be replaced by other suitable ones. A few guidelines for acquainting people with unfamiliar songs may be helpful:

1. Identification through imitation

First try to sing any song in its original language in order to sense the beauty and the intricate text-tune relationship; then sing the translation. Through the language and the music of a culture one can get a glimpse of that specific culture, and the music will make it easier to struggle with the unfamiliar language. By imitating we can identify ourselves at least a little with one another. Songs may draw us into other social realities of justice and peace work, into different vocations of doxology and praise, into a new experience of the self-emptying love of Jesus or a cry for mercy. It is important to try to be as faithful as possible to the original style of the music. For example, to maintain the simplicity and integrity of songs from other parts of world, Western harmonization should not be used.

2. Assistance of local immigrants

In many places today it is possible to find immigrants from different parts of the world who might be invited to help teach the pronunciation and intonation of words.

3. The role of the choir

A choir is generally the most effective instrument for implanting new congregational songs. All songs should thus be well known and well rehearsed by the choir, and it may be helpful to form a local ecumenical choir for this purpose.

4. The role of the animator

Learning new songs will always be much easier if there is a song leader, an animator, with good teaching skills, aesthetic sensibility, musical imagination and enthusiasm.

5. Songs need to be rehearsed

New songs in worship always need to be practised before the service begins. If time allows, some essential information about the songs and their background can also be provided. This is a good way to build up an atmosphere of corporate togetherness in the congregation.

6. Repetition is the mother of pedagogics

Songs need to be sung over and over again in order to be known and loved. The short sung acclamations are designed for repetition, and they are usually learned quickly and easily, which is especially an advantage where people have difficulties in reading music or texts. A pastor once remarked to me how prayer intermingled with short sung responses had given the services in his congregation a new flexibility. "We were only used to singing hymns, with their intellectual approach to doctrine. The framework was stiff and prayer was separated from the hymns. Now we have learned that music can be an essential part of our praying."

7. Music involves the body

Many songs from Africa and Latin America are sung with body movements. In order to get many people to move with the music, it is not enough to tell them to move. The animator, perhaps with the help of the choir, has to show people *how* to move. It is easiest to begin by getting people to move their feet.

8. Different music requires different instruments

Try to find instrumentalists acquainted with the different styles of music. In most urban areas there are African drummers, Latin American guitarists skilled in the sometimes complex rhythms of South America or instrumentalists familiar with some of the wide range of Asian music. If original instruments are not available, substitutes will also work — sounds on a synthesizer, regular flutes or hand-clapping (for drums). Much of the music used within the ecumenical movement is also sung a cappella (without accompaniment).

9. The role of the Holy Spirit

Emotion, feeling, senses and the movement of the Holy Spirit are vital to the process .of learning new songs.

THE WORSHIP SPACE

Liturgical words are not enough in the shaping of a living liturgy. Whatever attracts the eye has an important role in liturgy. While some traditions devote a lot of work to shaping the space of worship, in others it is almost neglected. The ideal is a separate place, exclusively used for worship, in which one is free to move, to change, to create. The experience of doing worship in a multi-cultural ecumenical setting has shown that several factors are important:

— *Make the space as beautiful as possible*. Many elements can be used for this: an altar, a cross, candles and votive candles, icons and other spiritual pictures, flowers, hangings.
— *Make the space as ecumenical as possible*. Even when the worship takes place in a church, it may be possible to make small changes or additions that can reduce some of the sometimes strong denominational character.
— *Make the space as participatory as possible*. Make sure there is enough room for processions, for symbolic actions, for the choir.
— *Let the theme of the specific service influence the look of the space*.

LEADERSHIP

The role of the worship leader is essential in making liturgy come alive, especially in a service in which many people are actively participating. It is often on the initiative of the local pastor or worship leader that new ways of worshipping are tested and implanted in the local setting, and his or her personal perseverance and enthusiasm are usually the basis of making this work. Ecumenical experience has shown that the worship leader needs to:

— *take the initiative* (or to be open to initiatives taken by others) for implanting ecumenical worship in the local context;
— *coordinate* the planning, rehearsal and finally the celebration of the service;
— *be well prepared,* knowing all the details of the service;
— *be devoted to his or her task*;
— *create an atmosphere of security and confidence* in a situation where many might feel uncertainty, for liturgy is the rejoicing play of God's children before the face of their God;

— *leave space for others* and their spiritual gifts;
— *show respect* for all participants, all traditions and all expressions of Christian faith;
— *be open* to the surprising work of the Holy Spirit.

USING SYMBOLS

Many would consider the use of symbols and participatory symbolic actions as one of the most fascinating and enriching elements in ecumenical worship. At the same time it has often aroused strong feelings and even evoked deep theological questions.

Symbols and symbolic language have always been an essential part of the Christian faith. According to Paul Ricoeur, "there is more in a symbol than in any of its conceptual equivalents... Symbols give rise to an endless exegesis... No concept can exhaust the requirement of further thinking borne by symbols."[27] Jesus often used strong metaphors to speak of himself, like the familiar "I am" sayings in the gospel of John: "I am the bread of life..., the light of the world..., the good shepherd..., the true vine." Apocalyptic literature also features an abundance of deeply resonating symbols, including the powerful word-pictures of heaven in the book of Revelation: the river of the water of life, the tree of life... for the healing of the nations.

The language of symbols has been called "the language of the angels", "the first language of the faith" or the "mute Word". In medieval times, when most people were illiterate, the church was like a great picture-book, in which each detail had its deep meaning. Much of the art of interpreting these symbols has been lost, and only a few of them remain alive in modern times — the cross, the lamb, the dove. In Western Christian history the ear came to dominate over the eye. More and more, the Word was considered as something to be preached, taught and heard. Today there is a renaissance of visualization of the faith in a world dominated by the visual media. Experts in communications say that at least 75 percent of all the information that reaches people reaches them through the eyes.

The worship services in this book and the next section of this chapter offer some examples of how symbols and symbolic actions can be used ecumenically. Some have been harvested from the rich liturgical soil of different Christian traditions; others are new. Those using these and other symbols and symbolic actions in worship should remember four important points:
— The use of symbols demands a great deal of sensitivity to the different cultures and traditions of the worshippers. A symbol which communicates meaningfully to some people may strike others as artificial, distracting, funny or even embarrassing. Thus all symbols must be tested with people involved in the worship, to anticipate and eliminate any potential ambiguities.
— Any symbolic action must be carefully rehearsed beforehand with those involved in leading it.
— Worshippers should always be invited to take part in symbolic actions, not compelled.
— All liturgy, including symbols and symbolic actions, is for the benefit of the kingdom of God. Symbols are never an end in themselves.

EXAMPLES OF SYMBOLIC ACTIONS IN LITURGY

Mercy triumphs over judgment

Two consecutive morning services at a WCC meeting used the theme "Mercy triumphs over judgment". The services were celebrated outdoors in a small arena. The first used the texts from James 2:1-13 and Matthew 5:17-20. The text from James ends with the words "mercy triumphs over judgment". After the Bible readings — standing in judgment under the law of God — people were invited to reflect on personal or social failures or failures of the churches. They could confess these silently or make them visible by writing them on large sheets of paper posted on a wall at the front, which quite a few of the participants did. During this period of silent and written confessions, all sang a Kyrie. The concluding words of forgiveness pronounced to all were brief: "Hear the good news: The mercy of Christ triumphs over judgment!"

The next morning the papers had been taken down from the wall, cut into pieces and placed on the ground, with stones arranged around them in the shape of a cross. The texts from 1 John 3:11-18 and Matthew 5:21-26 were read, and after the Bible readings each participant received a flower. All were invited "to make peace with your neighbour by exchanging flowers as gifts of mercy, as signs of forgiveness. When you are reconciled to your neighbour, you may offer your gift by laying your flower on the cross." By the end of the worship the "failures" — written the day before — were covered by the flowers of mercy within the sign of the cross. Mercy triumphs over judgment!

The red thread — the blood of suffering and struggle

In 1993 liturgists and musicians from all continents met for a two-week seminar on art and liturgy sponsored by the Latin American Council of Churches (CLAI), the Institute for Religious Studies (ISER) and the WCC. Daily worship was planned, prepared and celebrated by the participants. Because of difficulties of interpretation they were asked to use as few words as possible.

One worship remained with the participants more than the others. It focused on something common to all people — blood, with a special emphasis on the blood of women. On the central altar, which was covered by a red cloth, were a Bible, candles and a basket with pieces of red yarn. The text from Mark 5:25-34 spoke of the woman "who had been suffering from haemorrhages for twelve years" and was healed by touching the cloak of Jesus. The litany remembered all the women in the world who are bleeding in suffering and pain.

> We remember the bleeding wounds of women working in factories and brothels... We remember women, our mothers, our sisters and our daughters, battered and bleeding in their homes by husbands and lovers. We remember this bleeding woman, who touched Jesus deeply. We have also been touched by the blood of a woman. Jesus acknowledged this woman, gave her life and risked solidarity with her — alone, unclean and marginalized...

As an act of solidarity all participants were invited to tie a red thread around the wrist of their neighbour and in so doing to remember the reconciling blood of Jesus and the women in their own lives who had touched them deeply. This tiny thread remained on the wrists of many participants during the rest of the seminar.

Prayer altars

In Helsinki, Finland, a liturgical revival has grown out of the longing of many people for authentic worship expressions in the setting of a large city. Thus the St Thomas Mass was created. Within this eucharistic liturgy there is a focus on prayer. During the first part, participants are invited to walk around in the church to eight different prayer altars, each with its own theme. At each altar one may write out a prayer and put it in a small basket and light a candle. The prayers are then collected and used in the common intercessory prayer. At the same time, those who wish may walk to the main altar where ministers and lay people are prepared to give personal prayers and even anoint people with oil. During the entire time devoted to this "prayer walk", songs are sung. This kind of participatory and corporate prayer action gives new life to old liturgical customs.

The cross

The cross is the strongest symbol in the Christian faith, a symbol of suffering and love, of death and life, of earth and heaven. It is the ultimate sign of the love of God, expressed through the suffering, death and resurrection of Jesus Christ. The death of Jesus on the cross tells us where God is. God does not escape evil. As an instrument of execution, the cross also reminds us of the suffering and tortured people of our own times. But on the cross Jesus overcomes evil. The cross turns into a sign of victory.

The cross is used in many forms of passion walks (one of which is described in this book, "Walking the way of the cross"). In the community of Taizé a large wooden cross is laid out on the floor in each Friday liturgy. People are invited to kneel by the cross, light a candle and meditate on the reconciliation of Christ. In some Christian traditions the cross is decorated by flowers and greenery at Easter in an act of turning a symbol of death into a tree of life.

Water

Water is the wellspring of all life. In our mother's body we rested and grew before birth, surrounded by the amniotic fluid. Clean water is a necessity for life. At the same time water can be dangerous and threatening. It can drown and destroy life. The powers of chaos are often described as large floods. Water as a symbol of both life and death is prominent in the biblical texts. In the Christian tradition this double meaning of water is best understood in baptism, in whose water we die with Christ and are reborn, cleansed and renewed with the risen Lord.

Water has always played an important part in all Christian liturgy. It can be used in liturgies of baptismal renewal, in the washing of feet in the Maundy Thursday worship, in blessings where water can be sprinkled, in liturgies focusing on the need for water on the earth. I recall an especially poignant use of water symbolism during a meeting of the committee that prepared worship for the Canberra assembly. The focus was on the tears of the world; and a bowl with salted water was circulated among us. We were invited to taste the salted water, remembering the tears of the world and our own tears. In doing so I suddenly and quite surprisingly realized how long it had been since I had actually wept. In reminding me of my lack of tears the salt water also pointed to my lack of compassion. Suddenly my tears came — tears of shame, tears of sorrow, tears of compassion — before the compassionate God, whose Son was able to weep. No words awakened me, no preaching, just the taste of salted water.

Stones

A stone manifests power. Stones endure and are difficult to destroy. In many cultures the stone evokes protection against harm and death. This idea of protection and permanence explains the use of stones on graves. In the Bible the stone is a sign pointing to God. God is not the rock, but the rock tells us something about God. The stone may also contain within it the song of life: "I tell you, if these were silent, the stones would shout out" (Luke 19:40). The temple of God is made up of living stones, of which the cornerstone is Jesus himself (1 Peter 1:5-8). But stones can also be used in hate and condemnation. "Let anyone among you who is without sin be the first to throw a stone at her" (John 8:7).

Liturgically, stones can be effectively used as part of the confession of sins. Each participant receives a stone at the beginning of the service as a sign of the weight of our sins, and in the confession the stones are handed over to the mercy of God. Stones are often beautiful and can be used in natural art forms for worship. For example as part of a service, an altar or meditation place can be built out of stones brought by each participant.

Candles

Light is another powerful biblical metaphor for God. "The Lord is my light and my salvation" (Ps. 27:1), "God is light and in him there is no darkness at all" (1 John 1:5). Jesus speaks of himself as "the light of the world" (John 8:12), but the people of God are also supposed to be "the light of the world" (Matt. 5:14) and we are supposed to live "as children of light — for the fruit of the light is found in all that is good and right and true" (Eph. 5:8-9).

As bearers of light, candles have always had an essential part in Christian liturgies. At Christmas and Easter candles are lit as a sign of the incarnation and resurrection. At Easter the large paschal candle (the light of Christ) is lit and is extinguished on Ascension Day. In many traditions baptismal candles are handed over to the newly baptized. Candles are lit in the churchyards in remembrance of the dead.

Candles can be used in intercessory prayers. One example comes from the St Hilda Community:

> There is always a bowl of sand, symbolic of the desert wilderness, set in the centre of the circle with a single lighted candle in its centre. Next to the bowl sits a basket of small votive candles. During the intercessions, people are free to light a candle from the basket and place it in the sand while naming, either silently or aloud, their petition or thanksgiving. Sometimes flowers are substituted for candles, and an empty vase is placed beside the bowl. The end of this section of the liturgy yields a bowl of light or a vase overflowing with flowers, reminding us of our collective humanity and of the light and beauty of God's response to us. [28]

In many liturgies of baptismal renewal, participants are invited to light candles as a sign of their renewal.

Conclusion

Worship is the meeting-place between the revealed God and the people of God. To worship is to reveal the Lord of the church, the risen Christ, and to reveal ourselves to God and each other. There is no contradiction between the mystery of God and the revelation of God, because the mystery of God is God's revelation. The incarnation is the innermost secret of this mystery. In the different liturgies of the church this mystery of incarnation is shaped. The languages, the symbols, the music, the gestures, the vestments, the architectures may differ, but everywhere the meeting between the living God and the people of God takes place. And we continue to learn from each other on our way towards the unity Christ is praying for.

The incarnation means that the Lord has become human in everything: in our laughter and in our crying, in our struggle and in our exhaustion, in our songs of praise and in our protest, in our orders and in our spontaneity, in the use of all our senses. We meet this incarnated God in our worship, together, despite all limits and barriers, in many languages, in words and actions for the sake of life.

A sense of inviting openness to tradition, renewal and the worldwide community of Christians is vividly captured in the introduction to the song book of the Pilgrim Church in South Australia:

> Welcome to Pilgrim
> and to the community that worships here.
>
> Here we seek
> to honour God who calls us to worship,
> personally and corporately,

child, youth and adult,
to be free to wonder and be still (in body and spirit),
to create in word, music and movement,
to relate to people here and beyond, and
to make new our relationship with God.
Please come among us as one of us...

Our music is mostly contemporary,
often original and part of us.
We hope it will bring joy and meaning and richness
as it becomes familiar.
Through it we are linked to other people
and communities around the world...

We seek in our worship to state again,
with our understanding and our feeling,
the old and new truths of the gospel.

Involvement and participation are at the heart of our worship.
When you are ready to contribute to its planning, please offer.

The life of this worshipping community continues through our
lives as we are the church in the world.

Let us wait,
expecting to meet the living God.[29]

NOTES

[1] Suzanne Fageol, *Women Included: A Book of Services and Prayers*, London, SPCK, 1992, p.16.

[2] Gail Ramshaw-Schmidt, "Naming the Trinity: Orthodoxy and Inclusivity", *Worship*, vol. 60, no. 6, Nov. 1986, p.491.

[3] Rosemary R. Ruether, "The Feminist Liturgical Movement", in *A New Dictionary of Liturgy and Worship*, London, SCM Press, 1986, p.240.

[4] Fageol, *op. cit.*, p.22.

[5] *Ways of Worship: The Report of a Theological Commission of Faith and Order*, London, SCM Press, 1951.

[6] *Drumbeats from Kampala*. Report of the first assembly of the All Africa Conference of Churches, London, Lutterworth, 1963, pp.35-36.

[7] Norman Goodall, ed., *The Uppsala Report*, Geneva, WCC, 1968, p.81.

[8] Tom Best and Janet Crawford, "Praise the Lord with the Lyre... and the Gamelan?", *The Ecumenical Review*, Jan. 1994, p.80.

[9] *Let's Worship: A Handbook for Worship*, Geneva, WCC, 1975, p.8.

[10] David M. Paton, ed., *Breaking Barriers, Nairobi 1975*. Official report of the fifth assembly of the WCC, Geneva, WCC, 1976, p.8.

[11] Pablo Sosa, in the "Memoir" of the art and liturgy seminar, Rio de Janeiro, Feb. 1993, Geneva, WCC-JPIC, 1993, p.4.

[12] Best and Crawford, *op. cit.*, p.90.

[13] Michael Kinnamon, ed., *Signs of the Spirit*. Official report of the WCC's seventh assembly, Geneva, WCC, 1991, p.120.

[14] Ivor H. Jones, *Music: A Joy for Ever*, London, Epworth, 1989, p.8.

[15] Anders Nyberg, ed., *Freedom Is Coming: Songs of Protest and Praise from South Africa*, Uppsala, Utryck, 1984, p.4.

[16] *New Hymns for a New Day*, Geneva, WCC, 1966, pp.6-9.

[17] Robin A. Leaver, "Theological Dimensions of Mission Hymnody", in Vernon Wicker, ed., *Hymnology International*, vol. 1, 1991, p.40.

[18] D.T. Niles, *The Message and its Messengers*, New York and Nashville, Abingdon, 1966, p.105.

[19] I-to Loh, "Toward Contextualization of Church Music in Asia", *Journal of Theology*, IV/1, 1990, p.296.

[20] *Sound the Bamboo: CCA Hymnal*, Quezon City, Philippines, CCA, 1990. The "Editor's Notes", pp.17-18, offer some additional suggestions about singing Asian songs.

[21] Desmond Tutu, in the foreword to *Amandla 3: We Shall Never Die*, Uppsala, Utryck, 1986, p.2.

[22] Tom Colvin, *Fill us With Your Love, and Other Hymns from Africa*, Carol Stream, Illinois, Agape, 1983, pp.3-4.

[23] Nyberg, *op. cit.*, p.6.

[24] Ivor H. Jones, *op. cit.*, p.9.

[25] Frederick Wilson, ed., *The San Antonio Report*, Geneva, WCC, 1990, p.111.

[26] *The Iona Community Worship Book*, Glasgow, Wild Goose Publications, 1988, pp.8-9.

[27] Paul Ricoeur, *Interpretation Theory*, 1976, p.57.

[28] Fageol, *op. cit.*, pp.20-21.

[29] *Songs for the People of God*, printed in 1992 by Pilgrim Church, 12 Flinders St, Adelaide, South Australia 5000.

● A special word of thanks must go to my good ecumenical friend Terry MacArthur, worship consultant for the World Council of Churches. Without his invaluable work at every stage — not only the considerable task of editing and typesetting all the music but also his support through ideas, suggestions and sharing of liturgical experience — this book would never have been published.

1. Worship Services
in the Perspective of Mission

In early summer 1989 700 persons from all over the world came together in San Antonio, Texas, USA, for the conference on world mission and evangelism organized by the Commission on World Mission and Evangelism (CWME) of the WCC. The theme of the conference was "Your Will Be Done — Mission in Christ's Way". A worship committee had worked for almost two years on planning the conference worship life. The committee's mandate was "to plan for participatory, inclusive worship, which would enable a large group of participants to worship as one across confessional, cultural and linguistic lines". Within that mandate the team was concerned to integrate the worship life with the programmatic discussions of the conference and to deepen the understanding and exploration of the conference theme through participation in a liturgical life of prayer, song, readings and actions.

And it was in the daily worship services that the conference became a family, gathering each morning in the university chapel. Each day the attendance grew as more and more recognized this was no ordinary opportunity to sing and to pray. The services all followed a similar structure; within that pattern there was variety of movement and language, of people and symbolic actions. Because no interpretation was possible in the chapel, there was a minimum of spoken words during the time of reflection. The orders of services were printed each morning in the four official languages and many other languages were used in the singing, prayers and readings.

The central and biblical image of growth with its rich imagery of planting, nourishing, pruning, waiting for the harvest and gathering the fruit, provided continuity as well as a central focus for the worship. In order to make the focus both individual and corporal, the worship committee decided to use one specific symbol through most services: for the individual focus, it was a small wooden bowl from Haiti with different contents each morning; and for the corporal, it was big clay pots in which the growing of the seed was visible. Eight hundred small bowls had thus been prepared by local wood-carvers in Haiti, and participants were given one at the closing worship as a reminder of their personal commitment to "mission in Christ's way". In each service there was a Bible procession ("the entrance of the Word"), where the Bible was carried by one of the readers, accompanied by two people carrying candles.

In this section are the eight services that were held on the biblical image of mission: a seed that falls to the ground and dies in order to bear much fruit.

Though the services were planned with a continuous flow of biblical images on the same theme, each one can stand on its own in a local context. For a week-long meeting or less, the services "Every branch that bears fruit is pruned" and/or "Behold how the farmer waits for the land to yield its crops" can be omitted.

Bowls usable in local settings may be ordered from a local potter — or perhaps borrowed from the kitchen of your church. The local gardener may be able to provide the large pots.

Flowers Will Bloom in the Wilderness

In the chapel there were five big clay pots, one in the front and four by the entrance (smaller settings would require less) All the pots were already filled with some soil. When participants arrived, each received a small bowl with soil. In the silences during the moment of reflection some participants had previously been asked to deposit their soil in the pot standing in the front. At the end of the service all were invited to empty their bowls into one of the pots and to leave their bowls in the chapel.

* * *

Song Rehearsal

Silent Preparation

(Each participant has been given a small bowl of soil to focus personal and communal reflection on preparation for "the way of the Lord")

Call to Worship (stand)

Leader: The desert will sing and rejoice,
flowers will bloom in the wilderness;
streams of water will flow,
the burning sand will become a lake;
all will see the Lord's splendour,
see the Lord's greatness and power.

Song: *(soloists or the choir may sing the verses and all join in the refrain)*

Pablo Sosa: Argentina

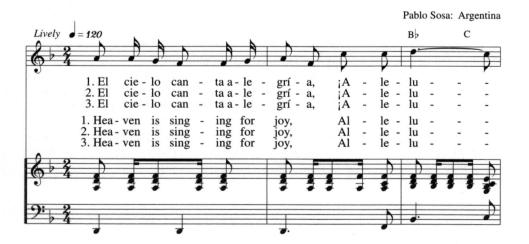

ya! por - que en tu vi - da y la
ya! por - que a tu vi - da y la
ya! por - que tu vi - da y la

ia! for in your life and in
ia! for both your life and
ia! for both your life and

mí - a bri - lla la glo - ria de Dios.
mí - a las u - ne el a - mor de Dios.
mí - a pro - cla - ma - rán al Se - ñor.

mine is shin - ing the glo - ry of God.
mine u - nite in the love of God.
mine will al - ways bear wit - ness to God.

Refrain

¡A - le - - lu - ya, A - le - lu -
Al - le - - lu - ia, Al - le - lu -

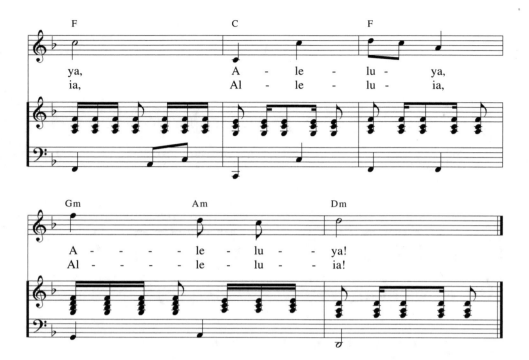

Melody, Spanish and English © Pablo Sosa, Camacuá 282, 1406 Buenos Aires, Argentina. Accompaniment, Terry MacArthur © 1994 WCC.

Call to Prayer

Leader: Before the world existed,
People: God was.

Leader: Before the light shattered the darkness
         and the sea burst from its womb,
People: God was.

Leader: In the uncertainty of all new beginnings,
People: God was, God is, God will be.

Prayer (sit)

Leader: Let us pray —
         with Abraham and Sarah,
         who did not know where they would go;
         with Moses and Aaron,
         who did not know what they should say;
         with Ruth and Naomi,
         who did not know what they would do;
         We depend on your grace and guidance, O God.

Response: *(sung a cappella; low basses may sing the bottom note an octave lower)*

Ky-ri-e e-lei-son, Ky-ri-e e-lei-son, Ky-ri-e e-le - - i-son.

Leader: Because you alone are God
and all our righteousness is like filthy rags;
Because you are the God of all beginnings,
who waters the dry land and causes the desert to bloom;
Because you are the source and author of life –
we depend on your grace and forgiveness, O God.

Response: Kyrie eleison

Silent prayer

Leader: God is good.
God offers forgiveness to those who truly repent,
and promises the joy and freedom of the Holy Spirit
to all who believe.
Thanks be to God.
People: Amen.

Entrance of the Word (stand) *(sung a cappella or with drum)*

First time-Leader; Repeat-All

Glo - ria   a   Dios,   Glo - ria   a   Dios,   Glo - ria   en   los   cie - los!
Glo - ry   to   God,   Glo - ry   to   God,   Glo - ry   in   the   high - est!

A   Dios   la   glo - ria   por   siem - pre!   Al - le - lu - ya,   A - men!
To   God   be   glo - ry   for - e - ver!

Al - le - lu - ya,   A - men!   Al - le - lu - ya,   A - men!

2. Gloria a Dios, Gloria a Dios,
   Gloria a Jesucristo. . .

2. Glory to God, Glory to God,
   Glory to Christ Jesus. . .

3. Gloria a Dios, Gloria a Dios,
   Gloria sea al Espíritu. . .

3. Glory to God, Glory to God,
   Glory to the Spirit. .

Old Testament Reading: Isaiah 35:1-8a

Response: Glory to God

Reflection (sit)

Leader: We are gathered at this conference [meeting/service] to pray that God's will be
          done among us — on earth, as in heaven. The prophet Isaiah has given us a
          vision of what God will do among us: "Flowers will bloom in the wilderness!
          The desert will sing for joy!" In the coming days let us enact and, in so doing,
          participate in God's mission of making flowers bloom out of the dry land — out
          of the wilderness of individual lives, of communities and of our world. Let us
          participate in the planting, the growing and the bearing of the fruit of the
          message of the gospel in all of life. Today we prepare together the soil; let us
          remember that it was in the desert that the word of God came to John the Baptist:
          "Prepare the way of the Lord".

Voice: We bring to you the wastelands of the earth, O God:
          — the no-hope places, where oppression and injustice rule,
          — the deserts where people die of hunger and thirst,
          — the earth, depleted and devastated by human greed,
          — the soil, that will not yield.
          Because these things should not be so, we cry aloud:
          Your kingdom come, O Lord.

(Silence, during which the soil is deposited in the pot by some participants)

Response *(sung a cappella)*

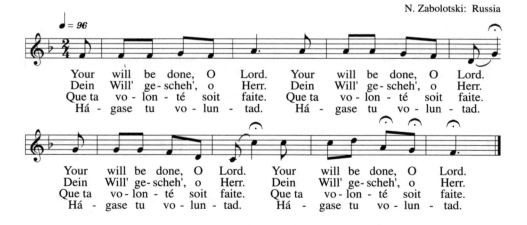

N. Zabolotski: Russia

Your	will	be	done, O	Lord.	Your	will	be	done, O	Lord.
Dein	Will'	ge-scheh',	o	Herr.	Dein	Will'	ge-scheh',	o	Herr.
Que ta	vo-lon-té	soit	faite.		Que ta	vo-lon-té	soit	faite.	
Há-gase	tu	vo-lun-tad.			Há-gase	tu	vo-lun-tad.		

Your	will	be	done, O	Lord.	Your	will	be	done, O	Lord.
Dein	Will'	ge-scheh',	o	Herr.	Dein	Will'	ge-scheh',	o	Herr.
Que ta	vo-lon-té	soit	faite.		Que ta	vo-lon-té	soit	faite.	
Há-gase	tu	vo-lun-tad.			Há-gase	tu	vo-lun-tad.		

Voice: We bring to you the wastelands of our life in community,
          — the parishes where hope has died,
          — the missions that have lost their vigour,
          — the councils that fear and suspect change.
          Because these things should not be so, we cry aloud:
          Your kingdom come, O Lord.

(Silence, soil is deposited)

Response: Your will be done, O Lord.

Voice: We bring to you the wastelands of our lives,
— when faith and hope are in dust and ashes,
— when the fruit of the Spirit is not in evidence,
— when love does not find expression in our lives.
Because these things should not be so, we cry aloud:
Your kingdom come, O Lord.

(Silence, soil is deposited)

Response: Your will be done, O Lord

Leader: Prepare a way, O Lord, in the desert, in our deserts,
for Christ to come and make all things new.

Lord's Prayer (in your own language)

Benediction (stand)·

Leader: May the love of God enfold us.
People: May the grace of God uphold us.

Leader: May the power of God set us free
People: to love and serve all God's people.

Leader: Now to God, who by the means of the power working in us,
is able to do so much more than we can ask or even think;
to God be glory in the church and in Christ Jesus for all times,
for ever and ever.
People: Amen.

Song

S. Dauermann: USA

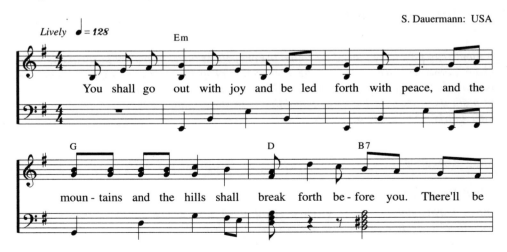

Lively ♩ = 128

Em

You shall go out with joy and be led forth with peace, and the

G   D   B7

moun-tains and the hills shall break forth be-fore you. There'll be

shouts of joy and the trees of the field shall clap, shall clap their hands, and the trees of the field shall clap their hands, and the trees of the field shall clap their hands, and the trees of the field shall clap their hands and you'll go out with joy.

Unless a Seed Falls into the Ground and Dies...

A number of pots were placed all round the chapel. At the entrance all participants were given a bowl with seeds. At the time of reflection people were asked to gather round the pots in small groups with their bowls and at the end of the reflection they were all invited to plant their seeds in the large pots filled with soil. Again people were asked to leave their bowls when going out of the chapel.

* * *

Song Rehearsal

Silent Preparation

(Each participant has been given a small bowl with seeds, to focus personal and communal reflection on the mystery of life out of death)

Call to Worship (stand)

Leader: From before the world began
         and after the end of eternity,
People: you are God.

Leader: From the sea bursting out its womb
         to the wind ceasing from its chase,
People: you are God.

Leader: In the constancy of created things
         and in their fickleness,
People: you are God.

Leader: In the vastness of the universe
         and the forgotten corners of our hearts,
People: you are our God, and we bless you.

Song

W. Barnard: Netherlands

Frits Mehrtens: Netherlands

1. De   aar - de   is   ver - vuld   van   goe - der - tie - ren - heid,
1. The   whole earth   is   ful - filled with   God's for - bear - ing   mind,
1. Pour   ren - dre grâce   à   Dieu   qui   chan - te - ra   le   mieux?

van   god - de - lijk ge - duld   en   god - de - lijk be - leid.
full   of   a   god - ly   grace and   sym - pa - thy di - vine.
Ceux   qui, sans hé - si - ter   cher - chent sa vo - lon - té

2. Gods goedheid is te groot
voor het geluk alleen,
zij gaat in alle nood
door heel het leven heen.

3. Zij daalt als vruchtbaar zaad
tot in de groeve af
omdat zij niet verlaat
wie toeven in het graf.

2. God's goodness is too great
for happiness alone,
it goes through deepest pain,
bred in our very bone.

3. It penetrates as seed
into the furrow's womb
because it does not leave
the sleepers in the tomb.

2. Dieu parle en ses travaux:
on peut le prendre au mot,
il a dressé son plan
qu'il mène au long des temps.

3. Le vent souffle où il veut:
il reste aux mains de Dieu.
L'homme a conquis le ciel,
seul Dieu est éternel.

4. Omdat zij niet vergeet
wie godverlaten zijn:
de wereld hemelsbreed
zal goede aarde zijn.

5. De sterren hemelhoog
zijn door dit zaad bereid
als dienaars tot de oogst
der goedertierenheid.

6. Het zaad der goedheid
   Gods,
het hoge woord, de Heer,
valt in de voor des doods,
valt in de aarde neer.

7. Al gij die God bemint
en op zijn goedheid wacht,
de oogst ruist in de wind
als psalmen in de nacht.

4. Because it does not rest
until the lost are found,
sky-wide, the world becomes
a fair and fruitful ground.

5. The stars above, sky-high,
are by this seed prepared,
as servants sent to reap
the mercy of the Lord.

6. The seed of godly love,
the Lord, the world of truth,
descends into the earth,
into the soil of death.

7. All you, in love with God,
who for this goodness wait,
the grain waves in the wind
as psalm tunes in the night.

4. Dieu reste le plus fort
quand il vainc notre mort:
pour le Dernier combat,
c'est Dieu qui fait le poids.

5. On peut compter sur lui,
il n'a jamais trahi
ceux qui se sont fiés
à sa fidélité.

6. Dieu rit des Importants
qui croient en leur Argent:
si tu t'avoues petit,
il prendra ton parti.

7. C'est le Vivant Seigneur
qui nous tient en son cœur
plus vaste que le temps:
sa gloire nous attend.

Music and Dutch © Interkerkelijke Stichting voor het Kerklied, Pijnacker, Holland. English, © 1974 Fred Kaan, reproduced by permission of Stainer & Bell, Ltd. P.O. Box 110, 23 Gruneisen Road, London N3 1DZ, England. French, Daniel Hameline © Centre national de pastorale liturgique, 4, Avenue Vavin 75006 Paris, France.

Call to Prayer (sit)

Voice: Jesus said: "The kingdom of heaven is like this: A man takes a mustard seed and sows it in his field. It is the smallest of all seeds, but when it grows up, it is the biggest of all plants. It becomes a tree, so that birds come and make their nests in its branches." (Matt. 13:31-32)

Silence

Leader: "Remember not the former things.
Do not consider the things of old.
Behold I am doing a new thing;
now it springs forth — do you not perceive it?" (Isa. 43:18-19a)

People: Lord, we await;
do a new thing among us....

Leader: "For a long time I kept silent;
I did not answer my people.
But now the time to act has come;
I cry out like a woman in labour." (Isa. 42:14)

People: Lord, we await;
do a new thing among us...

Leader: "Who would have believed what we now report?
Who could have seen the Lord's hand in this?
It was the will of the Lord that his servant
should grow like a plant taking root in dry ground." (Isa. 53:1-2)

People: Lord, we await;
do a new thing among us...

Leader: What is sown in the earth as a perishable thing is raised imperishable.
Sown in humiliation, it is raised in glory;
sown in weakness, it is raised in power;
sown as physical, it is raised as spiritual. (1 Cor. 15:42-44a)

People: Lord, we await;
do a new thing among us...

Leader: Let us pray:
Eternal God, fount of all wisdom, the giver of life;
so fill our hearts with hope
that in our doubts and despair
we would learn to wait upon you.
Sow in us the seeds of your love
that we learn to die with Christ
and so share the glory of his resurrection.

People: Amen.

Entrance of the Word (stand)

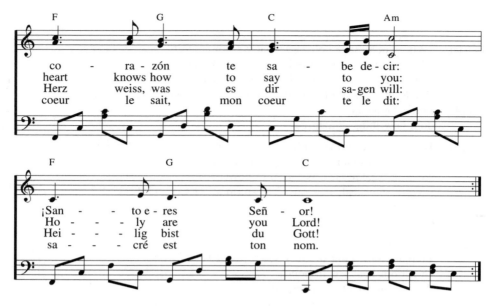

German, Wolfgang Leyk. French, Joëlle Gouël © 1990 WCC.

Old Testament Reading: Isaiah 55:10-11

Response: Santo, santo, santo

Gospel Reading: John 12:23-26

Leader: This is the word of the Lord.
People: Thanks be to God.

Reflection (sit)

Solo: Unless a grain of wheat shall fall *(see the recessional song)* (sit)

(While the soloist sings people move to stand in small groups around the large bowls, holding their own bowls of seeds)

Leader: Eternal God,
    your Word declares that the life which is laid down in faith
    will be raised and produce a great harvest.
    This we celebrate as we proclaim:
People: Christ has died, Christ is risen, Christ will come again.

Leader: We remember and praise you
    for the saints and martyrs of this and every age.
    We name them before you now.

(Remaining where they are standing, people are invited to name saints and martyrs)

Leader: These lives, like seeds, dropped to the ground;
          yet their witness has borne fruit and enables us to say:
People: Christ has died, Christ is risen, Christ will come again.

Leader: We pray for your church throughout the world
          and for that part to which we belong,
          that it may be ready to spend and to be spent in your service,
          that the love of self-preservation may be set aside,
          that the deaths you demand of it may be embraced joyfully,
          and that through all it may proclaim:
People: Christ has died, Christ is risen, Christ will come again.

Leader: In silence,
          we surrender ourselves and all that we count important
          to your will and purpose.
          For we cannot know the glory of Christ's resurrection
          if we do not have the fellowships of sufferings.
          And we cannot expect to gather the kingdom's harvest
          if we do not sow the kingdom's seed.

(You are invited to plant your seeds in the large bowls)

Leader: In us and through us, may your Spirit proclaim:
People: Christ has died, Christ is risen, Christ will come again.

Lord's Prayer (in your own language)

Benediction

Leader: May the God of love, who loves us freely,
          strengthen us in our love for others;
          may Jesus Christ, who gave his life for us,
          grant us grace to give our lives for others;
          may the Spirit, who dwells in us,
          empower us to live for others.
People: Amen.

Recessional Song

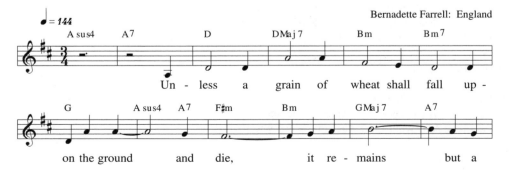

Bernadette Farrell: England

♩ = 144

A sus4   A7   D   DMaj7   Bm   Bm7

Un - less   a   grain   of   wheat   shall   fall   up -

G   A sus4   A7   F♯m   Bm   GMaj7   A7

on the ground   and   die,   it   re - mains   but   a

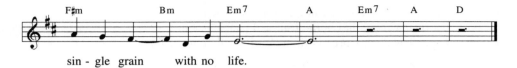

sin - gle grain   with no   life.

Like a Tree Planted by Rivers of Water

For this service there were five large pots in different places in the chapel, each containing a small plant. On entering the chapel all participants were handed a small bowl with either some water or a votive candle in it. During the scripture reading one participant poured water on the plant in one of the pots and a candle was lit in front of it. During the recessional singing people were invited to walk by one of the pots, either to water the plants or to light their votive candles and place them around the pot as a symbol of their participation in mission in Christ's way. During the three parts of the "call to worship" three actions took place: after people had answered, "And there was light", a candle was lit in the front of the chapel; after people had answered, "And what God was, the Word was", a drumbeat was heard; after people had answered, "He was one of us", a processional cross was brought to front of the chapel.

* * *

Song Rehearsal

Silent Preparation

(Each participant has been given a bowl either with water or with a candle to be used in the action of nourishing new life)

Call to Worship (stand)

Leader: In the beginning,
　　　　　when darkness was on the face of the deep
　　　　　and the Spirit of God brooded over the waters,
　　　　　God said, "Let there be light".
People: And there was light.

(A candle is lit)

Leader: In the beginning,
　　　　　when it was very quiet, God spoke.
People: And what God was, the Word was.

(Drumbeat)

Leader: When the time was right,
        God sent the Son. He came among us.
People: He was one of us.

(A cross is brought to the front of the church)

Song

Ramon & Sario Oliano: Kalahan Psalm 24:1   Ikalahan melody: Philippines

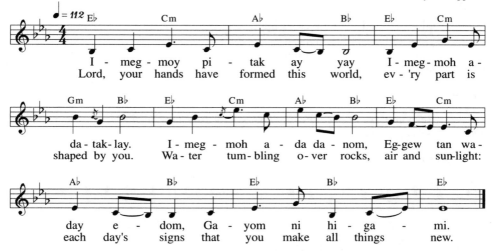

I - meg - moy   pi - tak   ay   yay   I - meg - moh   a -
Lord, your hands have formed this world, ev - 'ry part is

da - tak - lay.   I - meg - moh   a - da   da - nom,   Eg - gew   tan   wa -
shaped by you.   Wa - ter   tum - bling   o - ver rocks,   air and   sun - light:

day   e - dom,   Ga - yom   ni   hi - ga - mi.
each day's signs that   you   make all things new.

2. Pantaneman ipitak
Taklay i mangitodak,
Danom i an manibog,
Eggew i on dada od
Gayom ni hi-gami.

3. Botil i impad-agmi
Intanemmiday obi,
Dakel i ilamehda,
Manok, killom timmaba,
Gayom ni hi-gami.

4. Ambel-at i kayabang
Tep obimi aateng.
Dakel iday manokmi,
Tan matabay killomi,
Gayom ni hi-gami.

5. Mik anapay inom-an
Et waday panlamonan.
Mek anapay nemnemni
Anggan iday baholmi,
Gayom ni hi-gami.

2. Yours the soil that holds the seed,
you give warmth and moisture, too.
Sprouting crops and blossom buds,
trees and plants:
the seasons' signs that you make all things new.

3. Sweet potatoes fill our bags,
when the garden yields its due.
Chickens run, and pigs grow plump,
children too:
your bounty sings that you make all things new.

4. We search out new ground to weed,
even mountain fields will do.
You uproot the toughest sins
from our souls:
both steward signs that you make all things new.

5. Like a mat you roll out land,
space to build for us and you
earthly homes, and better still,
homes for Christ,
the truest sign that you make all things new.

Music and Ikalahan Words, Ramon and Sario Oliano, © Delbert Rice. English, Delbert Rice adapted by James Minchin © The Asian School of Music, Worship and the Arts, P.O. Box 10533, Broadway Centrum, Quezon City 1112, Philippines.

Call to Prayer (sit)

Leader: Jesus said: "I am the light of the world.
         Whoever follows me will have the light of life
         and will never walk in darkness."

People: He is our light.

Leader: Jesus said: "The water that I will give will become
         a life-giving spring within and give eternal life."

People: He is the water of life.

Cantor: Glory to God, who gives us light,
         glory to God in the highest,
         and on earth may peace reign
         among people of good will.

Prayer

Response (*sung a cappella; basses may sing text on the note of C sustained throughout*)

Russia

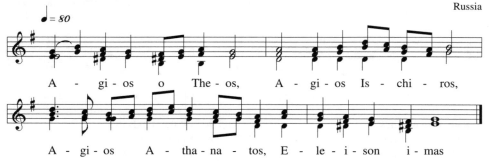

Holy God, Holy Mighty, Holy Immortal: have mercy on us.

Leader: Maker of Light and lover of humankind,
         we praise you for every truth, insight and discovery
         by which our lives have been enriched.
         But above all we worship and adore you
         for sending to earth your Son.
         He is the light of the world,
         and all earth's darkness will never put him out.

         Response: Agios o Theos

Leader: O, God, you have opened to us the sea of your mercy
         and watered us with full streams
         from the riches of your grace
         and the springs of your kindness.
         Kindle in us the fire of your love,
         sow in us your fear,
         strengthen us in our weakness,
         and bind us close to you and to each other.

Response: Agios o Theos

Leader: We confess, O living God,
that when the light of Christ has burned brightest
we have sometimes found darkness more alluring;
that though you have asked us to let our light shine,
we have sometimes hidden it.

People: Lord, have mercy.

Leader: Like a tree planted by rivers of water,
our lives have been nourished
by the faithfulness of your love;
but we have sometimes betrayed your goodness
by refusing a cup of water to a stranger.

People: Lord, have mercy.

Leader: Depending not on our virtue, nor on our faith,
but solely on your grace,
we seek your pardon and ask for your peace.

People: Lord, have mercy.

Leader: Listen, for this is what God has promised:
"A new heart I will give you
and a new spirit I will put within you.
You shall be my people and I will be your God."

People: Amen. Thanks be to God.

Entrance of the Word (stand)

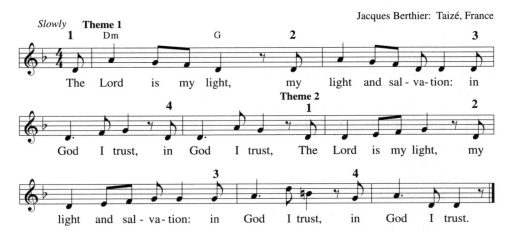

Le Seigneur est ma lumière et mon salut. En lui je me confie.
Der Herr ist mein Licht und mein Heil. Auf ihn vertraue ich.
El Señor es mi luz y mi salvación. En él confío.

Reflection

Leader: Sisters and brothers, we are here gathered together in order to affirm our
participation in mission in Christ's way; to pray that God's will be done in our
lives and in the lives of all peoples. In the gospel, our Lord speaks of his life as
given for our nourishment. Nourishing lives with the water and the light of life
so that the seed of truth may take root in all hearts is part of our calling in
mission. As we read the scripture, we will water the plant and provide it with the
symbol of the light of life. At the close of the service we invite you to come
forward to pour water or to light your candle as a symbol of your participation in
mission in Christ's way.

Old Testament Reading: Isaiah 44:2-4 *(during the reading water is poured on the plant
and a candle is lit and placed in front of the pot)*

Leader: This is the word of the Lord
People: Thanks be to God.

Silence

Leader: Let us pray:
Eternal God, you are the water of life and the light of life;
by your grace you sustain and nourish the universe.
May the seed of your kingdom which you have planted,
grow and flourish for the good of all people
and the healing of the nations.
People: Amen.

Intercession (sit)

Leader: Where ignorance, self-love and insensitivity
have fractured life in community,
People: give your light, O God of love.

Leader: Where injustice and oppression have broken
the spirit of peoples,
People: give your light, O God who frees.

Leader: Where hunger and poverty, illness and death
have made life an unbearable burden,
People: give your light, O God of grace.

Leader: Where suspicion and hatred, conflict and war
have challenged your goodness,
People: give your light, O God of peace.

Leader: Eternal God,
remove the blindness of the nations and peoples
so that they may walk in the light of love;
remove the ignorance and stubbornness of nations and peoples
so that they may drink from the fountains of your goodness.
People: Amen.

Lord's Prayer (in your own language)

Benediction (stand)

Leader: The Lord bless us and keep us;
         the Lord's face shine upon us,
         and give us peace, this day and for ever.
People: Amen.

Song *(sung a cappella)*

(During the singing, people move towards the large bowls, either to water the plant or to light their candles, placing them around the bowls as a symbol of their participation in mission in Christ's way)

South Africa

Arrangement Anders Nyberg © Utryck, Klockargarden, Mossel, S-780 44 Dala-Floda, Sweden. US rights, Walton Music, 170 N.E. 33rd Street, Fort Lauderdale, Fl. 33334, USA.

Every Branch That Bears Fruit Is Pruned

By now the small plant had "grown" into a tree standing in a pot in the front of the chapel. A small tree (or a big branch) might be obtained from the local gardener or might even be found in woods nearby. No bowls were handed out. Instead, all participants received paper and a pencil. During the actual pruning of the large tree at the front (branches were cut off), participants were invited to write down what should be pruned in their own lives, in their societies and in the world. In the recessional, the pruned branches were carried out of the chapel and cast into a fire; participants then cast their written "prunings" into the same fire.

* * *

Song Rehearsal

Silent Preparation

(Each participant has been given a pencil and paper for use in the "pruning" action)

Call to Worship (stand)

Leader: Jesus said: "The kingdom of God is like this. A man scatters seed in the field. He sleeps at night, is up and about during the day, and all the while the seeds are sprouting and growing. Yet, he does not know how it happens...!" (Mark 4:26-27)

Silence

Leader: The work of God surrounds us!
People: We respond with praise.

Leader: The love of the Lord is visible!
People: We respond with joy.

Leader: The wind of the Spirit is moving!
People: We respond in hope.

Silence

Leader: O God, how marvellous are all your works;
People: in wisdom you have made them all.

Leader: Your constant love reaches above the heavens;
People: your faithfulness touches the skies.

Leader: We will sing your praises among the nations;
People: we will speak of your wonderful works among the peoples.

Hymn (*unison with drumbeat*)

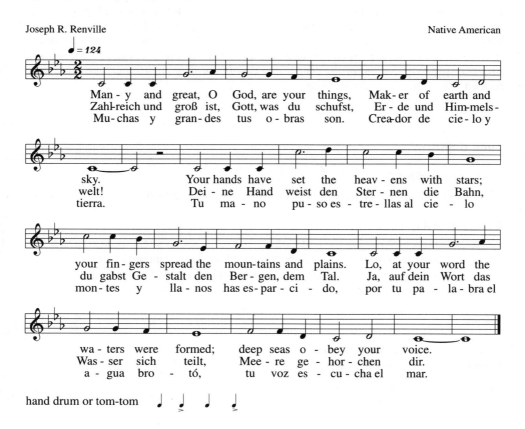

Joseph R. Renville   Native American

Man - y and great, O God, are your things, Mak- er of earth and
Zahl-reich und groß ist, Gott, was du schufst, Er - de und Him-mels-
Mu- chas y gran- des tus o - bras son. Crea-dor de cie - lo y

sky. Your hands have set the heav - ens with stars;
welt! Dei - ne Hand weist den Ster - nen die Bahn,
tierra. Tu ma - no pu - so es - tre - llas al cie - lo

your fin - gers spread the moun-tains and plains. Lo, at your word the
du gabst Ge - stalt den Ber - gen, dem Tal. Ja, auf dein Wort das
mon - tes y lla - nos has es - par - ci - do, por tu pa - la - bra el

wa - ters were formed; deep seas o - bey your voice.
Was - ser sich teilt, Mee - re ge - hor - chen dir.
a - gua bro - tó, tu voz es - cu - cha el mar.

hand drum or tom-tom

2. Grant unto us communion
    with you,
you star abiding one;
come unto us and dwell
    with us;
with you are found the
    gifts of life.
Bless us with life that has
    no end,
eternal life with you.

2. Wir bitten, gib'
    Gemeinschaft mit dir,
du bist das Licht, das bleibt.
Komme zu uns und
    wohne bei uns,
du hältst des Lebens
    Gaben bereit.
Segne mit Leben,
    das nie vergeht,
das ewig lebt bei dir.

2. Que entre nosotros
    tu siempre estés
Sé tú el principal
En medio nuestro ven a morar
contigo esté el don de le vida
Bendícenos con vida sin fin
Vida eterna en ti.

English, paraphrased by Philip Frazier. German, Dieter Trautwein © Strube Verlag GmbH, Pettenkoferstr. 24, D-80336 München, Germany. Spanish, Juan A. Gattinoni.

Call to Prayer (sit)

Leader: Sisters and brothers, the seed that falls into the ground sprouts and grows into a tree! This is the Lord's doing; it is marvellous in our eyes. But this promise of growth and of bearing fruit is accompanied in scripture by the warning that every branch that does not bear fruit is cut off and cast into the fire. Every branch that bears fruit is pruned. Pruning is a necessary part of growing; it is also God's action, so that the plant may bear much fruit. Let us pray.

    Silent prayer

Voice: "Come, everyone who is thirsty — here is water!
Come, you that have no money — buy corn and eat!
Why spend money on what does not satisfy?
Why spend your wages and still be hungry?" (Isa. 55:1-2)

Leader: Eternal God,
remove from our lives our false confidence
and dependence on things that do not belong to the kingdom;

People: and teach us to abide in your love.

Voice: "When you lift up your hand in prayer,
I will not look at you.
No matter how much you pray,
I will not listen to you...
Wash yourselves clean.
Stop all this evil that I see you doing...
Help those who are oppressed;
give orphans their rights." (Isa. 1:15-17)

Leader: Loving God,
remove from our lives false religion –
the religion of the self
which does not reach out to the others,

People: and teach us to abide in your love.

Voice: "What shall I bring to the Lord, the God of heaven,
when I come to worship him...?
Will the Lord be pleased if I bring
thousands of sheep or endless streams of olive oil...?
No, the Lord has told us what is good.
For what he requires of us is this:
to do what is just, to show constant love,
and to live in humble fellowship with our God." (Mic. 6:6-8)

Leader: Gracious God,
remove from us everything that leads to injustice and oppression
in our societies,

People: and teach us to abide in your love.

Leader: Teach us to remember, O God,
that you have called us to work, to live and to die
in the service of your kingdom.
Remove from us everything that stands in the way
of your will for us.

People: Amen.

Entrance of the Word (stand)

Iona Community: Scotland

♩ = 108

I am the vine and you the bran-ches, pruned and prepared for all to see; chose-en to bear the
fruit of hea-ven if you re-main and trust in me.

Words and music, John Bell © 1988 Wild Goose Resource Group, The Iona Community, Pearce Institute, Govan, Glasgow G51 3UU, Scotland.

Gospel Reading: John 15:1-4

Response: I am the vine

Continuation of the Reading: John 15:5-8

Response: I am the vine

Reflection (sit)

Leader: Sisters and brothers, the scriptures remind us that everything that does not
belong to God's will should be removed so that life might bear fruit. As we
prune this tree, I invite you to write down on the sheet provided what you know
should be pruned and cast into the fire — in your life, in our several societies
and in our world. At the close of the service we will proceed out of the chapel
and cast our sheets of paper into the bowl of fire.

(Silence, during which the tree is pruned and people write)

Prayer (stand)

Leader: O God, give us courage for you have called us to pull down,
to cut off and to tear down.

Response

Dinah Reindorf: Ghana

© 1988 Dinah Reindorf, P.O. Box 13060, Accra, Ghana.

Leader: Give us love,
for you have called us to build, to plant and to nurture.

Response: Kyrie eleison

Leader: Give us discernment
to know when you will us to act and to know how to act in faithfulness.

Response: Kyrie eleison

Leader: Give us humility
so that all that we do may be done for your glory
and for the sake of your kingdom.

Response: Kyrie eleison

Lord's Prayer (in your own language)

Benediction

Leader: O God, send us now in peace.
Help us to hold fast to that which is good.
Help us to return no evil for evil.
Help us to support the faint-hearted,
to uphold the weak and to honour all people.
And may the blessing of God,
who creates, redeems and sanctifies all life,
be with us all.
People: Amen.

Song *(sung a cappella)*

Nicaragua

En - via - do soy de Dios   mi ma - no lis - ta es - tá
Sent by the Lord am I,   my hands are read - y now
En - voy - é par Dieu.   Voi - là mes mains Sei - gneur

pa - ra cons - truír con él   un mun - do fra - ter - nal.
to help con - struct a just   and peace - ful, lov - ing world.
pour con - struire un monde   de jus - tice et de paix.

Behold How the Farmer Waits
for the Land to Yield its Crops

Everyone was able to see the tree in its pot. All participants were given an empty bowl. They joined in a litany of waiting with the prophets Isaiah and Jeremiah, Amos and Hosea, who believed that God is a God of justice; with the women of the Bible: Sarah, Hannah, Elizabeth and Mary, who looked forward to new life and new beginnings; and with Jesus in the garden, who asked his disciples to wait with him. Participants reflected on the relationship between emptiness and waiting. In the intercessional prayer people were invited to share different concerns, while everyone sang continuously "watch and pray".

* * *

Song Rehearsal

Silent Preparation

(Each participant has been given an empty bowl to focus personal and communal reflection on waiting)

Invocation (stand) *(accompanied by light drums)*

The Church of the Lord (Aladura), Yoruba, Nigeria

♩ = 112

Wa   Wa   Wa   E - mi - mi - mo,
Come,   O   Ho - ly   Spir - it   come.
Komm,   o   komm Hei - li - ger   Geist.
O   viens,   Es - prit,   viens,

Tenor solo

E - mi - o - lo - ye
O   wise   Spir - it   come.
du   Geist   der   Wahr - heit
Es - prit   de   sa - gesse

Wa   Wa   Wa   A - lag - ba - ra
Come,   al - might - y   Spir - it   Come,
Komm,   o   komm   du   Geist   voll   Kraft.
O   viens,   puis - sant   Es - prit,   viens,

a - lag - ba - ra - me - ta
al - might - y   Tri - ni - ty
du   Geist   der   Ei - nig - keit
Puis - san - te   Tri - ni - té

Wa - o   wa - o   wa - o.
Come,   come,   come.
Komm,   Komm,   Komm.
Viens,   viens,   viens.

E - mi - mi - mo.
O Spir - it,   come.
Hei - li - ger   Geist.
O Es - prit,   viens.

Yoruba and Music © The Church of the Lord (Aladura), P.O. Box 71, Sagamu, Remo, Ogun State, Nigeria.
Transcription and English paraphrase by I-to Loh, © 1986 WCC and the Asian School of Music, Liturgy and the Arts.
German, Wolfgang Leyk. French, Joëlle Gouël © 1990 WCC.

Leader: Up to present time, all of creation groans with pain,
like the pain of childbirth.
But it is not just creation which groans:
we who have the Spirit as the first of God's gifts
also groan within ourselves,
as we wait for God to make us children of God
and set our whole being free.

Response: Wa, wa, wa emimimo

Leader: It was by hope that we were saved;
but if we see what we hope for,
it is not really hope.
If we hope for what we do not see,
we wait for it with patience.

Response: Wa, wa, wa emimimo

Leader: Listen, the Lord is waiting to show you favour.
God yearns to have pity on you;
for the Lord is a God of justice.
Happy are those who wait on the Lord.

Song

Iona Community: Scotland   American traditional, arranged by John Bell

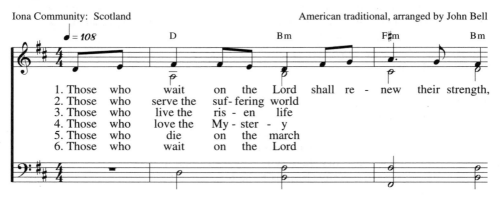

1. Those who wait   on the Lord shall re - new their strength,
2. Those who serve the suf- fering world
3. Those who live the ris - en life
4. Those who love the My - ster - y
5. Those who die   on the march
6. Those who wait   on the Lord

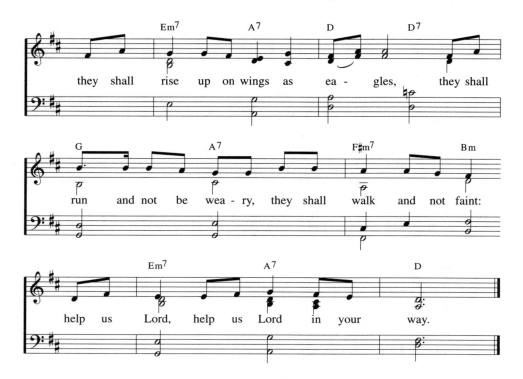

they shall rise up on wings as ea - gles, they shall run and not be wea - ry, they shall walk and not faint: help us Lord, help us Lord in your way.

Arrangement, John Bell and text © Wild Goose Resource Group, The Iona Community, Pearce Institute, Govan, Glasgow G51 3UU, Scotland.

Call to Prayer (sit)

Leader: The seed is sown; then we wait for it to grow. The plant grows; we wait for it to
bear fruit. We wait for God's action, for God's time, for God's will to be done.
Jesus asked the disciples to wait and pray with him. And the scripture proclaims:
"They that wait upon the Lord shall renew their strength, and mount up with
wings like the eagles."

Silence

Prayer

Leader: Let us pray:
Lord, your ways are not our ways;
your thoughts are not our thoughts;
what to us seems like eternity is only a moment to you.
In the face of eternity, help us to be humble.

Response *(sung a cappella)*

Iona Community: Scotland

Je - sus Christ,   Son   of   God, have   mer - cy   up - on   us.

Leader: If we have prayed only for what was possible
and hoped only for what we could see:

Response: Jesus Christ, Son of God

Leader: If we have taken your grace for granted
and expected instant answers to immediate requests:

Response: Jesus Christ, Son of God

Leader: If we have been patient when it seemed to our advantage
and impatient concerning the welfare of others:

Response: Jesus Christ, Son of God

Leader: If we have allowed waiting on your Spirit to slip into lethargy
and waiting on the kingdom to be replaced by apathy:

Response: Jesus Christ, Son of God

Leader: If we have only thought of us waiting on you
and never pondered how you wait on us:

Response: Jesus Christ, Son of God

Leader: Listen, for this is the true word of God:
blessed are all who wait for the Lord.
God is merciful, and God's love is sure and strong.

Lord, in these times,
should we fear that we are losing hope
or feel that our efforts are futile,
let us see in our hearts and minds
the image of your resurrection.
Let that image be the source of courage and strength.
In your company, help us to face challenges and struggles
against all that is born of injustice.
We ask this in Jesus' name.

People: Amen.

Entrance of the Word (stand) *(accompanied by drums or a rattle)*

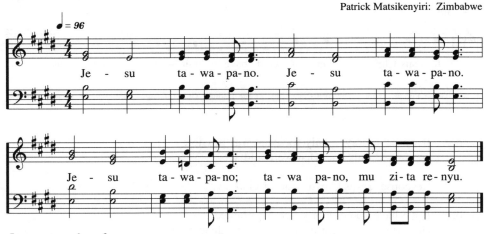

Patrick Matsikenyiri: Zimbabwe

Jesus, we are here for you.

Old Testament Reading: Psalm 40:1-5

Response: Jesu tawa pano

New Testament Reading: James 5:7-11

Response: Jesu tawa pano

Reflection (sit)

Leader: You have in your hands empty bowls. In some of the Asian religious traditions, emptiness is a subject for deep meditation. In silence let us meditate on the emptiness of the bowls in our hands. Paul speaks of Christ in the letter to the Philippians as someone who had "emptied himself"... Mary Magdalene saw the empty tomb... today we speak of empty stomachs... empty pews... What is the relation between emptiness and waiting?

Silence

Leader: Let us join in a litany of waiting.
With Isaiah and Jeremiah, Amos and Hosea and all the prophets,
believing that God is a God of justice,
People: we wait.

Leader: With Paul and Silas and all God's people,
imprisoned and persecuted for acting on their faith,
People: we wait.

Leader: With Naaman and Jairus, Bartimaeus and the Syro-Phoenecian woman,
         longing for an end to pain and rejection,
People: we wait.

Leader: With Zaccheus in his tree and the Samaritan widow at the well,
         keen to be liberated from a half-life,
People: we wait.

Leader: With Sarah and Hannah and Elizabeth and Mary,
         looking forward to new life and new beginnings,
People: we wait.

Leader: With Jesus in the garden, because he asks us to,
People: we wait.

Intercession *(sung a cappella) (While the song is sung softly and continuously, people are invited to rise and prayerfully share a concern; it does not matter if more than one person is speaking at once)*

Jacques Berthier: Taizé, France

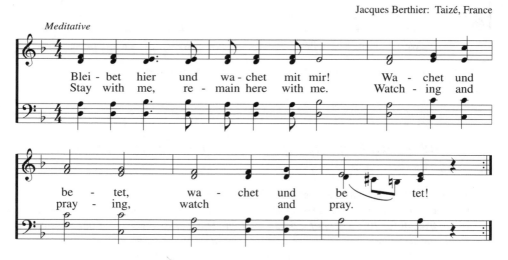

Music J. Berthier © Ateliers et Presses de Taizé, 71250 Taizé, France.

Lord's Prayer (in your own language)

Benediction

Leader: Lead us from death to life, from falsehood to truth,
         from despair to hope, from fear to trust.
         Lead us from hate to love, from war to peace.
         Let the peace that comes from hope fill our hearts.
People: Amen.

Leader: Listen, listen, says Jesus,
          I am coming, I am coming soon.

Response *(sung a cappella)*

Revelations 22:5, 20   Francisco F. Feliciano: Philippines

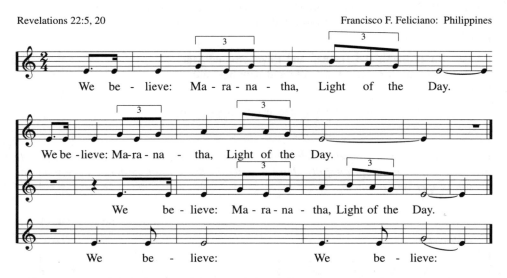

© The Asian School of Music, Worship and the Arts, P.O. Box 10533 Broadway Centrum, Quezon City 1112 Philippines.

The Fruits of the Spirit for the People of God

No bowls were handed out this morning. The seed sown in faith and nurtured in love, the plant pruned and tended with discernment, has born fruit. The seed of the gospel has borne the fruit of the furthering of God's kingdom. The fruit is the goal of our mission. At the front and around the fruit-giving tree a large quantity of fruits were laid out. At the end of the service people were invited to come to the front, take a fruit and share it with someone else as they walked to the Bible study which followed the service.

* * *

Song Rehearsal

Silent Preparation

Call to Worship (stand)

Leader: Out of chaos, you created order;
          out of darkness, you created light.

Response *(sung a cappella)*

Abraham Maraire: Zimbabwe

Leader: Out of eternity, you created time;
           out of the dust of the earth, you created life.

           Response: Hallelujah

Leader: Out of the desert you created a garden;
           out of the waters you created dry land.

           Response: Hallelujah

Leader: Out of a barren womb you produced a nation;
           out of the virgin womb you brought the Saviour.

           Response: Hallelujah

Leader: And in the fullness of time,
          the word was made flesh,
          walked, talked, lived, died
          and rose again among us...

          Silence

          Follow him — he is the way;
          believe him — he is the truth;
          love him — he is the life.

Hymn

Fred Pratt Green: England   Wales

1. For   the fruit   of   all cre - a - tion, thanks be to God.
2. In   the true   re - ward of la - bour, God's will is done.
3. For   the har- vests   of   the Spir - it, thanks be to God.

For   the gifts to   ev - 'ry na - tion, thanks be to God.
In   the help we   give our neigh- bour, God's will is done.
For   the good we   all in - her - it, thanks be to God.

For   the   plough - ing,   sow - ing,   reap - ing,
In   our   world - wide   task   of   car - ing
For   the   won - ders   that   as -   tound   us,

si - lent growth while   we   are sleep- ing,   fu - ture needs in
for   the   hun - gry   and   de - spair- ing,   in   the har - vests
for   the   truths that   still con- found us,   most   of   all that

earth's	safe-keep - ing,	thanks	be	to	God.
we	are shar - ing,	God's	will	is	done.
love	has found us,	thanks	be	to	God.

Words © 1970, Fred Pratt Green, reproduced by permission of Stainer & Bell, Ltd, P.O. Box 110, 23 Gruneisen Road, London N3 1DZ, England.

Call to Prayer (sit)

Leader: Sisters and brothers, in the Bible fruit is associated with aspects of our life and faith. Let us enter a period of prayerful meditation on the rich images that fruit brings to us.

Silence

Prayer

Voice: Then God said, "Let the land produce vegetation: seed-bearing plants and trees on the land that bear fruit with seed in it according to their various kinds." (Gen. 1:11)

Leader: Open our eyes to the wonder of your creation
and make us faithful stewards of your goodness.

Response *(sung a cappella)*

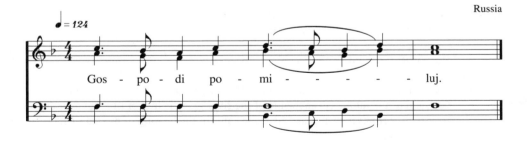

Voice: "She saw how beautiful the tree was and how good its fruit would be to eat… So she took some of the fruit and ate it… and he also ate it… and they realized that they were naked." (Gen. 3:6-7)

Leader: Help us, O God, in our wilful rebellion against your love.

Response: Gospodi

Voice: "The Lord your God brings you into a fertile land, a land of rivers and springs...
a land that produces wheat and barley, grapes, figs, pomegranates, olives and
honey... When you have all you want to eat and have built good houses to live
in... make sure that you do not become proud and forget the Lord your God who
rescued you from Egypt where you were slaves." (Deut. 8:7-8; 12-13)

Leader: Teach us, O God, not to forget your goodness
when life goes well for us.

Response: Gospodi

Voice: Jesus said: "A good tree cannot bear bad fruits, and a bad tree cannot bear good
fruits. You shall know them by their fruits."

Leader: Lead us, O God, not only to hear
but also do your will for the glory of your kingdom.

Response: Gospodi

Voice: "But the fruits of the spirit are: love, joy, peace, patience, kindness, goodness,
faithfulness, humility and self-control. And there is no law against these."
(Gal. 5:22)

Leader: Enable us to bear fruits, O God, so that people may see our good works and
praise you.

Response: Gospodi

Voice: Jesus said: "You have a saying, 'four more months and then the harvest'. But I
tell you, take a good look at the fields; the crops are now ripe and ready to be
harvested." (John 4:35)

Leader: Strengthen us in your service, O God,
so that we might always be in your mission.

Response: Gospodi

Voice: "And the angel showed me the river of the water of life... from the throne of
God and of the lamb. On each side of the river was the tree of life which bears
fruit twelve times a year... and its leaves are for the healing of the nations."
(Rev. 22:1-2)

Leader: Receive us, O God, in your love so that we may enjoy your presence with us.

Response: Gospodi

Leader: Eternal God, who raised Jesus Christ from the dead
as the first fruits of a new humanity,
help us to participate in the new life offered in him.

People: Amen.

Entrance of the Word (stand) *(verses may be sung by soloists or the choir and all join in the refrain; instruments: guitars, piano, flute and rhythm instruments)*

Guillermo J. Cuellar

Misa Popular Salvadoreña: El Salvador

F · Fine

de to - da la his - to - ria San - to San - to es nues - tro Dios.
Lord of all of his - tory, Ho - ly, Ho - ly is our God.
de tou - te l'his - toi - re, Très saint, Très saint, no - tre Dieu.
Herr uns 'rer Ge - schich - te, Hei - lig, Hei - lig, un - ser Gott.

F · Bb · C · F

Que a-com - pa - ña a nues - tro pue - blo, que vi - ve en nues - tras lu - chas, del
Who ac - com - pa - nies our peo - ple, who lives with - in our strug - gles, of
Qui ac - com - pa - gne son peu - ple char - gé de tous les far - deaux, u -
Er ist mit uns heut' und mor - gen, er lebt in un - serm Rin - gen, auf

C · F

u - ni - ver - so en - te - ro el ú - ni - co Se - ñor.
all the earth and hea - ven the one and on - ly Lord.
ni - que Sei - gneur de la ter - re, de l'u - ni - vers.
Er - den wie im Welt - all ist er al - lein der Herr.

Bb · C · F

Ben - di - tos los que en su nom - bre el E - van - ge - lio a - nun - cian, la
Bless - ed those who in the Lord's name an - nounce the ho - ly Gos - pel, pro -
Bé - nis soient ceux qui an - non - cent l'E - van - gi - le de la bon -
Lo - bet die in sei - nem Na - men das E - van - gel - ium kün - den, die

C7

bue - na y gran no - ti - cia de la li - be - ra - ción.
claim - ing forth the Good News: our li - be - ra - tion comes.
ne nou - vel - le de no - tre li - bé - ra - tion.
gu - te fro - he Bot - schaft: Be - frei - ung ist uns nah.

Introducción y Final

Gospel Reading: John 15:7-10

Response: Santo, Santo, Santo

Intercessions

Leader: Lord, loving God, maker of us all,
          help us to bear the fruits of the kingdom,
          for thorns do not produce grapes
          and figs do not produce thistles.

Response *(sung a cappella)*

Patrick Matsikenyiri: Zimbabwe

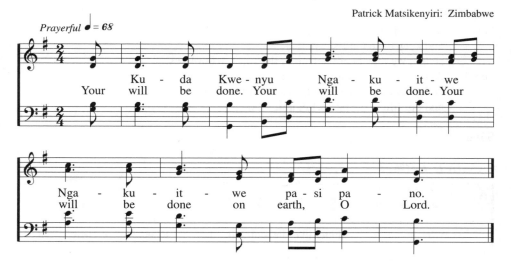

Leader: We pray for the nations of the world,
especially those in turmoil of conflict and war [nations are named].
Teach us peace, that we may bear the fruit of righteousness and love.

Response: Kuda Kwenyu

Leader: We pray for people who have been treated unjustly
or become victims of our social and economic systems.
Teach us compassion, that we may bear the fruit of justice.

Response: Kuda Kwenyu

Leader: We pray for all who seek to bring the message of love to those in need;
for those whose lives are spent in the service of others;
for all who are in mission — in Christ's way.
May your kingdom come,
and your will be done on earth.

Response: Kuda Kwenyu

Lord's Prayer (in your own language)

Leader: The seed sown in faith and nurtured in love, and the plant pruned and tended
with discernment, bears fruit. The seed of the gospel bears the fruit of the
furthering of God's kingdom. The seed of faith, nurtured by the Spirit, enables
us to bear the fruits of the Spirit in our lives. The fruit is the goal of our mission;
it is also the witness that our mission is done in Christ's way. Today we share
the fruit with each other as a sign of sharing all our gifts and lives, so that God's
will may be done on earth.

Benediction

Leader: May God bless us
and keep us in God's love
so that we may bear the fruit of the spirit in our lives.
People: And may God's warm welcome shine in our hearts
and Christ's peace prevail till our work is done
and our life made perfect in him. Amen.

Song

Roystonhill, arranged by John Bell: Scotland

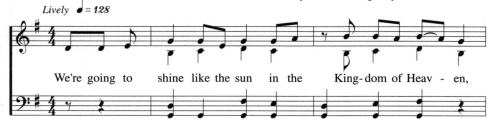

shine like the sun in the King-dom of Heav-en; we're going to

shine like the sun in the King-dom of Heav - en and

no one will ev-er be the same. And it's all in Je-sus'

name; and it's all in Je-sus' name; yes it's

all in Je-sus' name that no one will ev-er be the same.

2. We're going to learn from the poor
3. We're going to walk with the weak
4. We're going to drink new wine
5. And it all starts now

(During the second verse, people are asked to come down the centre aisle to the front and take fruit from one of the bowls, leaving by the side aisles. You are invited to share the fruit with each other as you leave)

Your Will Be Done — Mission in Christ's Way
(closing worship)

In the chapel the side walls were covered with trees made out of paper. When people arrived they were each given a bowl, which contained a green paper leaf and a pencil. In an act of thanksgiving they were all invited to write names of people "for whom we feel a special indebtedness" on the leaves and to put them on the trees around the walls. In the front again the tree was in focus, and around it were bowls with seeds. In the intercession all could offer their prayers. In receiving the Lord's blessing people were asked to raise their bowls. At the end of the service all participants were invited to go to the front and take seeds for their bowls. They were challenged to consider the seeds which God had sown within the conference, seeds of personal commitment to Jesus Christ, seeds that could bring new life to missions. The ending thus became a beginning also, the beginning of the liturgy after the liturgy. The exit from the chapel was also an entry into the world, to places of service and ministry, to mission in Christ's way. This worship is slightly adapted and shortened.

* * *

Gathering of the People

Call to Worship

Leader: The world belongs to God,
People: the earth and all its people.

Leader: How good and how lovely it is
People: to live together in unity.

Leader: Love and faith come together,
People: justice and peace join hands.

Leader: If the Lord's disciples keep silent
People: these stones would shout aloud.

Leader: Lord, open our lips
People: and our mouths shall proclaim your praise.

Processional Hymn *(sung a cappella)*
Sanna, sannina (South Africa), or
Sanctus and benedictus (p. 142)

Litany of Adoration (stand)

Leader: Glory to you, Almighty God!
              You spoke and light shattered darkness,
              order rose from confusion;
Women: You breathed into the dust of the earth
              and we were formed in your image;
Men: You looked on the work of your hands
              and declared that it was all good;

Leader: And still you speak, breathe and look for us.
All: We praise you!

Leader: Glory to you, Jesus Christ!
              You met us as a refugee, a threatened child,
              the Word made flesh, born in a forgotten place;
Women: You called us by name, to leave what was comfortable,
              to be your disciples, companions and friends;
Men: You saved us by kneeling at our feet,
              stretching your arms wide to take away our sins,
              walking through death to life again;

Leader: And still you meet, call and save us.
All: We praise you!

Leader: Glory to you, Holy Spirit!
              You brooded over chaos,
              mothering and shaping God's new creation;
Women: You inspired prophets and evangelists
              to discover the right word for the right season;
Men: You liberated the early church for mission,
              claiming all of life for the Lord of All.

Leader: And still you brood over, inspire and liberate us.
All: We praise you!

Leader: Glory to you, God, Three-in-One!
              You are surrounded by the song of the saints in heaven,
              and you are present with us now.
All: We adore you!

Hymn

The Iona Community: United Kingdom

Praise my soul (J. Goss)

♩ = 120

Praise with joy the world's Cre - a - tor, God of
Gloi - re soit à Dieu, le Pè - re Dieu de

jus - tice, love and peace, Source and end of hu - man
jus - tice et d'a - mour, Qui ré - pand sur no - tre

know - ledge, Force of great - ness with - out cease. Cel - e -
ter - re Vie et biens, jour a - près jour. Sour - ce

brate the Fa - ther's* glo - ry - Power to res - cue and re - lease.
de tou - te sci - en - ce, Il est fi - dèle à ja - mais.

2. Praise the Son who feeds the hungry,
frees the captive, finds the lost,
heals the sick, upsets religion,
fearless both of fate and cost.
Celebrate Christ's constant presence--
Friend and Stranger, Guest and Host.

2. Gloire au Fils qui nous libère
de la faim, de nos prisons,
retrouve celui qui erre
et l'accueille en sa maison.
Sa présence nous fait vivre
et donne la guérison.

3. Praise the Spirit sent among us,
liberating truth from pride,
forging bonds where race or gender,
age or nation dare divide.
Celebrate the Spirit's treasure--
foolishness none dare deride.

3. Gloire à l'Esprit qui rassemble
tous les hommes dispersés,
leur apprend à vivre ensemble
divers dans leur unité.
Corps du Christ, signe des cieux,
promesse d'un monde heureux!

4. Praise the Father*, Son and Spirit,
one God in Community,
calling Christians to embody
Oneness and diversity.
Thus the world shall yet believe when
shown Christ's vibrant unity.

4. Gloire soit à Dieu le Père,
le Fils et le Saint-Esprit,
un seul Dieu qui, sur la terre
nous appelle et nous bénit,
pour que l'unité vivante
soit pour tout homme un espoir!

*Originally Maker

Act of Repentance (sit)

Leader: Let us bow down before our God in prayer.

Response *(sung a cappella and in unison)*

© I-to Loh, Tainan Theological Seminary, 117 Section 1, Tung Men Road, Tainan, Taiwan.

Leader: If we have worshipped you as a relic from the past,
          a theological concept, a religious novelty,
          but not as the living God,
People: Lord, forgive us.

Leader: If our mission has been to the church
as if the cosmos did not matter,
or to the whole world,
as if our local situation did not matter,

People: Lord, forgive us.

Leader: If we have remained blind
to the gifts and insights of other believers,
and lived in a ghetto of the past
instead of the kingdom to come,

People: Lord, forgive us.

Leader: If we have confused your will with our understanding of it,
if we have preferred divergence to unity,
if we have sacrificed the gospel message on the altar of mass media,

People: Lord, forgive us.

Response: Ch'iu Chu

Leader: If we have heard stories of struggle
with no intention of sharing the burden of pain,

People: Lord, forgive us.

Leader: If we have identified the misuses of power
but failed to empower the weak,

People: Lord, forgive us.

Leader: If we have sung songs in praise of your creation
while defiling the goodness of the earth,

People: Lord, forgive us.

Response: Ch'iu Chu

Leader: If in our churches we have paid attention
to the liturgy, the preaching, the rituals,
with no thought for fellowship, interdependence or appropriate life-style,

People: Lord, forgive us.

Leader: If we have imitated the impersonal systems of the powerful,
rather than model ourselves on the communities of the poor,

People: Lord, forgive us.

Leader: If we have taken missionary initiatives with pride,
offered hospitality with reluctance,
or received the spiritual insights of others with suspicion,

People: Lord, forgive us.

Response: Ch'iu Chu

Leader: It is not because we have been faithful to our promise to follow,
but because you are faithful to your promise to forgive,
where repentance is real;
we ask for your word to pardon and restore us.

People: Forgive all our sins and receive us graciously,
and we will praise you as we have promised.
O God, show mercy to those
who have no one else to turn to.

Leader: The Lord says:
I will bring my people back to me.
I will love them with all my heart;
no longer am I angry with them.
I will be to the people like rain in dry land.
They will be firmly rooted like trees of Lebanon.
I will answer their prayers and take care of them,
like an evergreen tree, I will shelter them:
I am the source of all their blessings.
This is the promise of our God.
People: Amen. Thanks be to God.

Entrance of the Word (stand) *(sung a cappella)*

S.C. Molefe: Xhosa, South Africa

From the Lumko Song Book © Lumko Institute, P.O. Box 5058, 1403 Delmenville, Republic of South Africa.
English and transcription: Dave Dargie.

New Testament Reading: Colossians 3:12-17

Act of Thanksgiving

Leader: St Paul encourages us to give thanks at all times.
          This we do now, remembering before God
          those who have gone before us in faith,
          in the love and hope of God, in mission.
          Their names are all known to God, if not to us.
          But there are always particular people for whom
          we feel a special indebtedness,
          people whose faith and compassion
          has touched our hearts and maybe even changed our lives.
          Let us write their names on the paper leaves given to us
          as we entered. During the singing of the Caribbean Hallelujah
          we move to the trees around the walls
          and cover them with our leaves in gratitude to God.

Silence

Song

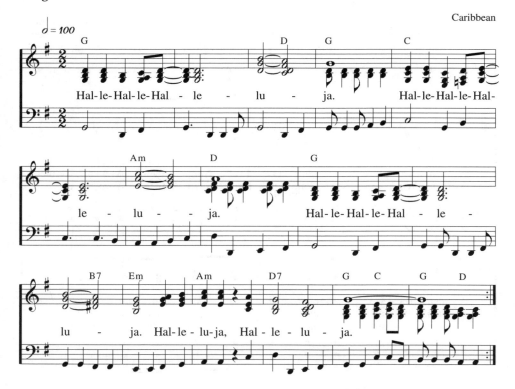

Arrangement, Terry MacArthur © 1994 WCC.

Gospel Reading: Luke 6:20-26

Response: Hallelujah

Prayers of Intercession

Leader: Sisters and brothers of Jesus Christ,
  in the beatitudes our Lord reminds us of the characteristics of God's kingdom
  and of the people who are blessed in God's will.
  Let us now offer our particular prayers which arise out of
  our experience, calling for God's goodness and mercy to come
  to the aid of the world's suffering people.

*(Prayers for troubled peoples and areas of the world are now offered. As the Kyrie is sung
quietly, those who wish are invited to rise and offer a short prayer aloud)*

Response: *(sung a cappella)*

Ky-ri-e e-lei-son, Ky-ri-e e-lei-son, Ky-ri-e e-le - - i-son.

Leader: Out of the depths we cry to you, O Lord,
  hear our prayer,
  awaken in us all the potentials
  which may become your means
  of answering the prayers of others.
People: In us, through us,
  and, if need be, despite us,
  may your will be done. Amen.

Lord's Prayer (in your own language)

Leader: Sisters and brothers, let us rise and join hands
  and pray the Lord's prayer together.

Song

Anders Frostenson: Sweden

Olle Widestrand: Sweden

2. Grenarna är många, stammen är en,
stammen - Jesus Kristus.
Grenarna är många, stammen är en,
vi är ett i honom.

3. Gåvorna är många, kärleken en,
finns i Jesus Kristus.
Gåvorna är många, kärleken en,
vi är ett i honom.

4. Tjänsterna är många, Anden är en,
Jesu Kristi Ande.
Tjänsterna är många, Anden är en,
vi är ett i honom.

5. Lemmarna är många, kroppen är en,
Jesu Kristi kyrka.
Lemmarna är många, kroppen är en,
vi är ett i honom.

2. Many are the branches of the one tree.
Our one tree is Jesus.
Many are the branches of the one tree.
We are one in Christ.

3. Many are the gifts giv'n, love is all one.
Love's the gift of Jesus.
Many are the gifts giv'n, love is all one.
We are one in Christ.

4. Many ways to serve God, the Spirit is one;
servant spirit of Jesus.
Many ways to serve God, the Spirit is one;
we are one in Christ.

5. Many are the members, the body is one;
members all of Jesus.
Many are the members, the body is one;
we are one in Christ.

2. Zweige wachsen viele aus einem Stamm.
Unser Stamm heißt Christus.
Zweige wachsen viele aus einem Stamm-
und wir sind eins durch ihn.

3. Gaben gibt es viele, Liebe nur eine.
Liebe schenkt uns Christus.
Gaben gibt es viele, Liebe nur eine-
und wir sind eins durch ihn.

4. Dienste leben viele aus einem Geist,
Geist von Jesus Christus.
Dienste leben viele aus einem Geist-
und wir sind eins durch ihn.

5. Glieder sind es viele, doch nur ein Leib.
Wir sind Glieder Christi.
Glieder sind es viele, doch nur ein Leib-
und wir sind eins durch ihn.

2. Muchas son las ramas, un árbol hay:
y su tronco es Cristo.
Muchas son las ramas, un árbol hay
y en él somos uno.

3. Muchos son los dones, uno el amor:
el amor de Cristo.
Muchos son los dones, uno el amor
que nos hace uno.

4. Muchas las tareas, uno el sentir:
el sentir de Cristo.
Muchas las tareas, uno el sentir
que nos hace uno.

5. Muchos son los miembros, un cuerpo hay:
ese cuerpo es Cristo.
Muchos son los miembros, un cuerpo hay
y en él somos uno.

Music © Olle Widestrand, Kälkbacksgatan 1, S-554 46 Jönköping, Sweden. Swedish Anders Frostenson © AF-Foundation Hymns and Songs/Verbum, S-104 65 Stockholm, Sweden. English © Estate of the late David Lewis, Bentham, Lancaster, LA2 7HL, England. Used by permission. German, Dieter Trautwein © Strube Verlag GmbH, Pettenkoferstr. 24, D-80336 München, Germany. Spanish © Pablo Sosa, Camacuá 282, 1406 Buenos Aires, Argentina.

Exchange of Peace

Leader: Lord Jesus Christ, you said to your apostles:
"Peace I leave with you, my peace I give to you."
Look not on our weakness,
but on the faith of your church,
and grant us your peace
for you live and reign forever and ever.
People: Amen.

Leader: The peace of the Lord be with you always.
People: And also with you.

(All exchange the peace)

Song: Wa, wa, wa emimimo (see pp.54-55) *(accompanied by light drums)*

Litany of Commitment

Leader: Sisters and brothers, let us stand and affirm what we have discovered
of God's will in the company of each other.
That we worship one God,
Father, Son and Holy Spirit,
in whose image we are made,
to whose service we are summoned,
by whose presence we are renewed,

People: This we believe.

Leader: That it is central to the mission of Christ
to participate, by word and action,
in the struggles of the poor for justice,
to share justly the earth's land and resources,
to rejoice in the diversity of human culture,
to preserve human life in all its beauty and frailty,
to witness to the love of God for all people of the earth,
and to invite all to share that converting experience,

People: This we believe.

Leader: That through the power of the Holy Spirit,
the persecuted shall be lifted up
and the wicked will fall,
the hesitant prayers and hidden actions of God's people
shall change the course of human history,
the ancient words of the scripture shall startle us with fresh insight,

People: This we believe.

Leader: That God has called the church into being
to be the servant of the kingdom,
to be a sign of God's new order,
to celebrate in the streets and fields of every land the liturgy of heaven,

People: This we believe.

Leader: That Christ, fully aware of our differences,
prays that we might be one
so that the world may believe,

People: This we believe,
and to this we are committed
for the love of God,
in the way of Christ,
by the power of the Holy Spirit. Amen.

Reflection (sit)

Leader: The bowls in our hands have made us reflect on the purposes of God in mission: how soil is prepared, the seed sown and nourished, the new plant pruned that in the fullness of time it may bear fruit. These bowls have been passed from hand to hand. We now take them home. Let us take them not empty, but holding seeds necessary for our mission in Christ's way. For a moment, let us consider what are the seeds which God has sown among us which we should take to bring new life to the mission, evangelism, social action and worship of our churches; and let us reflect on what seeds should be sown regarding our personal commitment to Jesus Christ.

Silence

(As the following are sung, all are invited to come forward carrying their empty bowls, receive seeds and return to their places)

Songs *(sung a cappella)*

Jacques Berthier: Taizé, France

Lento ♩ = 72

U - bi ca - ri - tas et a - - - mor.
U - bi ca - ri - tas et a - - - mor.

U - bi ca - ri - tas De - us i - bi est.
U - bi ca - ri - tas De - us i - bi est.

Music J. Berthier © Ateliers et Presses de Taizé, 71250 Taizé, France.

I am the vine *(sung a cappella)* (see p.50)

Benediction (stand)

Leader: Let us raise our bowls and receive the Lord's blessing.

> May the love of the cross,
> the power of the resurrection,
> and the presence of the Living Lord,
> be with you always.
> And the blessing of the Eternal God,
> Creator and Sustainer,
> Risen Lord and Saviour,
> Giver of holiness and love,
> be upon you now and evermore.

People: Amen.

Processional Song: Siyahamb' (see pp.45-46) *(sung a cappella)*

2. Services Using Water as the Central Image

Although we are not able to join together in the sacrament of baptism or a service of baptismal renewal, water remains a central image for our life together. Consequently, it is part of ecumenical worship. In some cases the references to baptism in the following services could be made more direct. The services come from three sources: a WCC executive committee meeting, the fifth world conference on faith and order, and the Canberra assembly.

Holy Spirit — Refresh Us with Living Water

The last part of this service is based on an Orthodox rite which is used mainly at Epiphany, but at other times also. This is not a service of baptismal renewal, but one in which all creation is summoned to participate in the sanctifying activity of the Holy Spirit.

Prior to Canberra, we used a similar service for a central committee meeting, but one with more references to baptism.

During the intercessions plenty of time should be allowed for the water to be poured. In Canberra the water was brought forward in glass bowls and poured into a large bowl on the altar. This action is an essential part of the prayer; it needs to be practised beforehand so that the participants are comfortable with it.

The prayer of blessing should be improvized or chanted on one note; it should not be hurried as it is full of biblical allusions.

While the choir and the congregation sing "When you, O Lord" the minister/priest can walk around sprinkling the congregation and the worship place as a sign of thanksgiving and blessing. A green branch can be used, and if the sprinkling is done with child-like delight, the service can become joyous and filled with grace.

At the end of the service people are invited to come and receive the water, which can be placed at the exits of the worship room. People may drink it or dip their hands in it. Some small cups (preferably not plastic) may be placed near the bowls. The final song is repeated while this action takes place.

* * *

Call to Worship (stand)

Leader: All who thirst, come to the water.
Come, all who are weary;
come, all who yearn for forgiveness.
The Holy Spirit through Jesus Christ has washed over us,
and our Gracious and Holy God beckons and blesses us.
Drink deeply of these living waters.

People: Glory to you, O Lord, glory to you.

Response

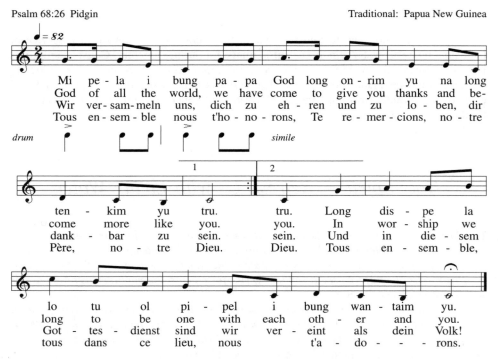

Psalm 68:26 Pidgin   Traditional: Papua New Guinea

♩ = 82

Mi pe-la i bung pa-pa God long on-rim yu na long
God of all the world, we have come to give you thanks and be-
Wir ver-sam-meln uns, dich zu eh - ren und zu lo - ben, dir
Tous en-sem-ble nous t'ho-no-rons, Te re-mer-cions, no-tre

drum   *simile*

ten - kim yu tru.   tru. Long dis-pe la
come more like you.   you. In wor - ship we
dank - bar zu sein.   sein. Und in die - sem
Père, no - tre Dieu.   Dieu. Tous en - sem - ble,

lo tu ol pi - pel i bung wan - taim yu.
long to be one with each oth - er and you.
Got - tes - dienst sind wir ver - eint als dein Volk!
tous dans ce lieu, nous t'a - do - - - rons.

© I-to Loh, Tainan Theological Seminary, 117 Section 1, Tung Men Road, Tainan, Taiwan. English © 1990 Fred
Kaan, Hazelwood Road 50, Acocks Green, Birmingham B27 7XP, UK. German, Dieter Trautwein © Strube Verlag
GmbH, Pettenkoferstr. 24, D-80336 München, Germany. French, Joëlle Gouël © 1991 WCC.

Leader: You are the fountain of life: refresh us.
          You are the cleansing spring: heal us.
          You are the well from which we drink and never thirst again:
          fill us.

          Response: Mi pela i bung

Litany of Confession (sit)

Leader: Lord and life-giving Spirit,
          who brooded over the waters when first the world began:
People: Make us dead to sin but alive to God.

Leader: Who led your people out of slavery
          through the waters of the Red Sea
          and into freedom through the waters of the Jordan:
People: Make us dead to sin but alive to God.

Leader: Who overshadowed Mary of Nazareth
and caused her to be the mother of God's only Son:
People: Make us dead to sin but alive to God.

Leader: Who anointed Jesus as Messiah
as he was baptized by John in the Jordan:
People: Make us dead to sin but alive to God.

Leader: Who raised Jesus from the grave
and proclaimed him Son of God in all his power:
People: Make us dead to sin but alive to God.

Leader: Who appeared in tongues of flame on Pentecost:
People: Make us dead to sin but alive to God.

Leader: Who charges the waters of baptism
through and through with power to give new life:
People: Make us dead to sin but alive to God.

Leader: Almighty and everlasting God,
who out of pure mercy decreed both the creation
and the renewal of the world.
Send forth the Spirit of adoption in full measure
that those who are born of water and the Spirit
may live under the power of that same Spirit all the days of their life
and so arrive safely in their heavenly home;
through Jesus Christ, our Lord.
People: Amen.

Entrance of the Word (stand)

Aleluia

© 1990 Simei Monteiro, Rua do Sacramento 230, Rudge Ramos CEP 09735-460, São Bernardo do Campo SP, Brasil.

Gospel Reading: John 5:1-4

Aleluia

Prayer of Intercession (sit)

Leader: Have mercy on us, God.
All creation is subjected to futility —
our futility, our folly which spoils, pollutes and poisons.
As your children, grant us that glorious liberty
which can set all creation free.
Let clean water come forth from the desert
and fresh streams in the wastelands until the trees of the field
clap their hands and the floods lift up their voice
in praise of your name.

(First pouring of water)

Response *(sung a cappella)*

G. M. Kolisi: South Africa

In 'ne-nce-ba' the middle syllable, 'nce,' is pronounced by making a 'tsch' sound that a mother uses to reprimand child, with the addition of a nasalized beginning.

Arrangement, Anders Nyberg © Utryck, Klockargarden, Mossel, S-780 44 Dala-Floda, Sweden. US rights, Walton Music, 170 N.E. 33rd Street, Fort Lauderdale, Fl. 33334, USA. French, Joëlle Gouël © 1991 WCC.

Leader: Have mercy on us, God.
We pray for all human beings, your creatures,
who thirst for life and who are often close to dying from thirst.
Grant them courage and hope in You
until that time when justice flows down like water
and righteousness like an everflowing stream.

(Second pouring of water)

> Response: Nkosi, nkosi

Leader: Have mercy on us, God.
As we gather together as Christians
remind us that we have passed through the waters of baptism.
Drown in us all that leads to division, prejudice and pride.
Refresh us by your Holy Spirit so that we may become a sign
of reconciliation and peace for the world.

(Third pouring of water)

> Response: Nkosi, nkosi

Blessing of the Waters (stand)

Leader: Blessed is our God, now and always,
and to the ages of ages.
People: Amen.

Leader: In peace let us pray to the Lord.

> Response: Gospodi pomiluj (see p.63) *(sung a cappella)*

Leader: That these waters may be sanctified by the power,
effectual operation, and descent of the Holy Spirit.
Let us pray to the Lord.
That there may descend upon these waters
the cleansing operation of the con-substantial Trinity.
Let us pray to the Lord.

> Response: Gospodi pomiluj

Leader: That this water may be a fountain welling forth unto life eternal.
Let us pray to the Lord.
That it may be for the healing of the souls and bodies
of all those who, with faith, shall draw and partake of it.
Let us pray to the Lord.

> Response: Gospodi pomiluj

Leader: Let us pray.
O Lord, by your will have you, out of nothingness,
brought all things into being and by your power
sustain all creation and by your providence direct the world.

You from the four elements have formed creation
and have crowned the cycle of the year with the four seasons;
all the spiritual powers tremble before you;
the sun praises you; the moon glorifies you;
the stars in their courses meet with you;
the light harkens unto you; the depths shudder at your presence;
the springs of water serve you;
you have stretched out the heavens as a curtain;
you have founded the earth upon the waters;
you have bounded the sea with sand;
you have poured forth the air for breathing;
the angelic powers minister unto you;
the choirs of archangels worship before you;
for you, being boundless and beginningless and unutterable,
did come down on earth, taking the form of a servant,
being made in the likeness of humans;
for you, O master, through the tenderness of your mercy,
could not endure the race of humans tormented by the devil,
but you came and saved us.
We confess your grace; we proclaim your beneficence;
we do not hide your mercy; all creation praises you,
who did manifest yourself,
for you were seen upon the earth, and did sojourn with us.
You hallowed the streams of the Jordan,
sending down from heavens your Holy Spirit,
and crushed the heads of dragons that lurked therein.
Therefore, O Lord, who loves humankind,
be present, you, yourself, now as then,
through the descent of your Holy Spirit and sanctify this water.

Response *(sung a cappella)*

A - men.

Leader: And through the partaking of this water,
through sprinkling it, wash away the defilement of passions.
We ask you now to visit our weaknesses and heal our infirmities
both of spirit and body through your mercy.
For you are our God, who through water and the Spirit renews our nature,
which had fallen into decay through sin.
For you are our God, who with water drowned sin in the days of Noah.
For you are our God, who by the sea, through Moses,
set free from slavery to Pharaoh the Hebrew race.

For you are our God, who cleaved the rock in the wilderness,
so that water gushed forth,
and who made the floods to well forth abundantly;
and satisfied your thirsty people.
For you are the fountain of healing, O Christ our God,
and to you we send up all glory,
together with your eternal Father and your all-holy,
good and life-giving Spirit,
both now and ever, and to the ages of time.

Response *(sung)*: Amen

Hymn *(sung a cappella)*

Not strict ♩ = *96*   Russia

When you, O Lord, were bap-tized in the Jor-dan,
the wor-ship of the Trin-i-ty was made man-i-fest.
For the voice of the Fa-ther bore wit-ness un-to you,
call-ing you the be-lov-ed Son, and the Spir-it in the form of a dove
con-firmed his word as sure and stead-fast.

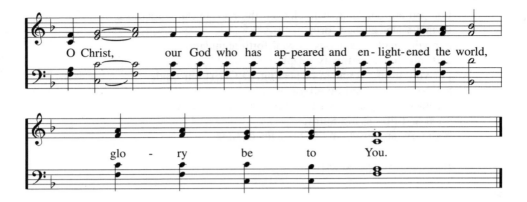

O Christ,   our God who has ap-peared and en-light-ened the world,

glo - ry   be   to   You.

(The priest sprinkles the altar with the blessed water. Then, moving among the people, the priest sprinkles the community, symbolizing the blessing of the nations and the world. All of creation participates in the sanctifying action of the Holy Spirit.)

Leader: Glory to you, O Christ, our God, our hope, glory to you.
People: Glory to the Father, and to the Son, and to the Holy Spirit,
            now and ever, and unto ages of ages. Amen.
            Lord, have mercy. Lord, have mercy. Lord, have mercy. Father bless.

Leader: May Christ our true God who for the sake of our salvation
            by his own will was baptized by John in the Jordan,
            through the prayers of his pure mother, our Lady,
            the Theotokos and ever-virgin Mary,
            by the power of the life-creating cross,
            and through the prayers of the prophet, forerunner and baptist John,
            of the glorious apostles, and of all the saints
            have mercy on us and save us, for he is good and loves humankind.

        Response (sung): Amen

Hymn: When you, O Lord

(The water should be placed by the exits and remain there for the whole day. The congregation is invited to partake of the blessed water.)

Living Water

A "river" painted on the floor ran right through the chapel, from the garden of Eden in front down to the baptismal font at the entrance, and out of the door. Most churches will not have such a painting but a "river" can be made with a long strip of cloth. The people were gathered at each side of the river. In the front on a small table was a glass bowl filled with water and a glass. Before the invocation the leader sipped the water as part of the prayer. During the last song, the bowl and glass were placed at the exit. As people went out, they could put their hand in the water and cross themselves if they wished.

* * *

Song

African American

1. O heal-ing riv - er, send down your wa-ters, send down your wa-ters up - on this land. O, heal - ing riv-er, send down your wa - ters
2. This land is parch-ing, this land is burn-ing, no seed is grow-ing in the bar-ren grounds. O, heal - ing riv-er send down your wa-ters.
3. Let the seed of free-dom a - wake and flour-ish. Let the deep roots nour-ish. Let the tall stalks rise. O, heal - ing riv-er, send down your wa- ters.

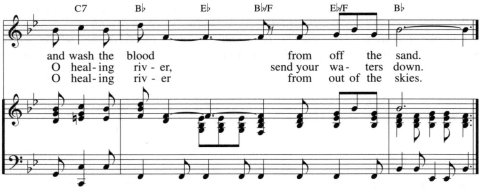

and wash the blood   from   off   the   sand.
O heal-ing riv - er,   send your wa - ters down.
O heal-ing riv - er   from out of the skies.

Arrangement, Terry MacArthur © 1994 WCC.

Invocation

Leader: With joy you will draw water
         from the wells of salvation.
People: Give thanks to the Lord, call on his name,
         make known God's deeds among the nations.

Leader: The living water will become a spring of water gushing up to eternal life.
People: Give us that water, so that we may never be thirsty.

Kyrie

Mt. Athos Melody: Greece

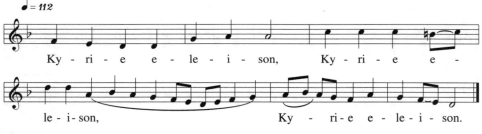

Ky - ri - e   e - le - i - son,   Ky - ri - e   e -
le - i - son,   Ky - ri-e e - le - i - son.

Lord, have mercy.

Silence

Leader: I take a sip of simple water.
         The atoms of the water are five thousand million years old.
         I drink the birth time of the earth.
People: We mourn with all living things that today carry the polluted water of creation.
         The salted tears in our eyes remind us of our origin and unity with all struggling
             life.
         Lord, have mercy.

Kyrie (sung)

Silence

Leader: I take a sip of simple water and with that the story of life.
Its molecules have been in the rain forest,
have lived in quantum compounds,
have waved in sea anemones,
have been the water of baptisms,
have lived in our mothers
and are now on their way to ever new formations.
People: With all living things we praise you, Lord Creator.
You are the well of salvation.

Song

Psalm 117:1   Jacques Berthier: Taizé, France

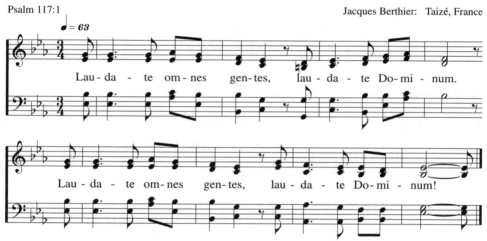

Lau - da - te om - nes gen - tes, lau - da - te Do - mi - num.

Lau - da - te om - nes gen - tes, lau - da - te Do - mi - num!

J. Berthier © Ateliers et Presses de Taizé, 71250 Taizé, France.

Epistle Reading: Revelations 22:1-7

Aleluia (see p.85)

Meditation

Prayer of Intercession

Leader: Have mercy on us, God.
All creation is subjected to futility —
our futility, our folly which spoils, pollutes and poisons.
As your children grant us that glorious liberty
which can set all creation free.
Let clean water come forth from the desert and fresh streams in the wastelands
until the trees of the field clap their hands
and the floods lift up their voice in praise of your name.

Response: Nkosi (see p.86)

Leader: Have mercy on us, God.
          We pray for all human beings,
          your creatures, who thirst for life
          and who are often close to dying from thirst.
          Grant them courage and hope in You
          until that time when justice flows down like water
          and righteousness like an everflowing stream.

Response: Nkosi

Leader: Have mercy on us, God.
          As we gather together this morning,
          coming from different traditions and churches,
          remind us that we have passed through the waters of baptism.
          Drown in us all that leads to division, prejudice and pride.
          Refresh us by your Holy Spirit so that we may become
          a sign of reconciliation and peace for the world.
People: Amen.

Lord's Prayer (in your own language)

Prayer of Thanksgiving and Blessing of the Water

Leader: Lord God, almighty, hear the prayers of your people:
          we celebrate our creation and redemption.
          Hear our prayers and bless this water
          which gives fruitfulness to the fields,
          and refreshment and cleansing to humanity.
          You made the water of baptism holy by Christ's baptism in the Jordan:
          by it you gave new birth and renewed us in holiness.
          May this life-giving element become the means of our refreshment
          and enable us to share the joy of all of nature,
          sanctified by Christ in his baptism.
          We ask this through Christ our Lord.
People: Amen.

Leader: All are invited, when leaving the chapel, to put a hand in the water, and perhaps
          make the sign of the cross, receiving refreshment and the Lord's blessing.

Benediction

Leader: The God, who created the waters of the world,
          the Son of living waters,
          the Spirit of cleansing waters be with you now and always.
People: Amen.

Song: O, healing river (see pp.91-92)

Recognition of Our Common Baptism

This was part of the daily services at the fifth world conference on faith and order held in Santiago de Compostela, Spain, in August 1993. One of the areas of progress which the faith and order movement has made possible is the recognition of our common baptism. Because we are not able to participate together in anything that resembles a sacrament, close connections with baptismal rites was avoided. In the courtyard of the seminary where we stayed was a large fountain. At the end of the service we processed down three flights of stairs to gather around this vivid image and sound of water. The choir was dispersed along the route so that the singing of the assembly was strengthened all the way. In local situations, such a service might process to a town well or fountain. If there are no sensitivities about sacramental sharing, this service could process to the font and the parts for a baptismal renewal could be included. Pastors might use some words which would recognize others' baptism.

* * *

Musical Preparation

Silence

Greeting (stand)

Leader: In Christ Jesus you are all children of God through faith.
As many of you as were baptized into Christ have clothed yourselves with Christ.

People: There is no longer Jew or Greek,
there is no longer slave or free,
there is no longer male and female;
for we are all one in Christ Jesus. Amen.

Prayer (stand)

Leader: Let us pray,
Almighty God, gracious Lord, pour out your Holy Spirit upon us. Keep us steadfast in your word, protect and comfort us in all temptations, defend us against all our enemies, and bestow on the church your saving peace; through your Son, Jesus Christ our Lord, who lives and reigns with you and the Holy Spirit, one God, now and for ever.

People: Amen.

Hymn

Christian David, Christian Gottlob Barth,
Johannes Christian Nehring

Bohemian Brethren: Germany

Son - ne der Ge - rech - tig - keit, ge - he
Je - sus, ra - diant sun so bright, let us
Christ, so - leil res - plen - dis - sant, lè - ve -

auf zu uns - rer Zeit, brich in dei - ner Kir - che an,
see a - gain your light. Shine with - in your church to - day,
toi sur no - tre temps, il - lu - mi - ne tous les cœurs,

dass die Welt es se - hen kann. Er - barm dich, Herr.
drive all dark - ness far a - way. Have mer - cy, Lord.
ma - ni - fes - te ta splen - deur! Dieu aie pi - tié.

2. Weck die tote Christenheit
aus dem Schlaf der Sicherheit;
mache deinen Ruhm bekannt
überall im ganzen Land,
Erbarm dich, Herr.

2. Bring your dormant church to life,
help us, Lord, in all our strife.
Let this land and every place
be a witness of your grace.
Have mercy, Lord.

3. Schaue die Zertrennung an,
der kein Mensch sonst wehren kann;
sammle, grosser Menschenhirt,
alles, was sich hat verirrt.
Erbarm dich, Herr.

3. See, your shattered church in need
finds no help but at your feet.
Gather, Shepherd, humankind,
all who_are lost and left behind.
Have mercy, Lord.

4. Tu der Völker Türen auf,
deines Himmelreiches Lauf
hemme keine List noch Macht.
Schaffe Licht in dunkler Nacht.
Erbarm dich, Herr.

4. Open wide new doors to preach,
till we all the nations reach.
Keep us steadfast in your might;
be our light in darkest night.
Have mercy, Lord.

2. Réveille-nous,
   tes croyants,
assoupis, indifférents,
fais entendre encore ta voix,
et convertis-nous à Toi.
Dieu aie pitié.

3. Qui peut rendre l'unité
à ton peuple divisé?
Berger de l'humanité,
réunis les égarés.
Dieu aie pitié.

4. Donne à tous tes messagers
la force et la charité.
Dans les larmes nous semons;
viens, fais croître la moisson.
Dieu aie pitié.

English, Erich Griebling, 1969. French © Georges Pucher, av. Rond-Point 2, 1225 Chêne-Bourg, Geneva, Switzerland.

Prayer of Confession (sit)

Leader: Through our baptism we live by faith that Christ now lives in us. We confess our failure to live in a manner worthy of Christ and of our calling. Therefore we call to you, our God.

People: What has happened to us? Where did we go astray?

Silence

Leader: In baptism you make us members of the body of Christ and call us into communion. We confess that we are hesitant to recognize each other's expressions of baptism; we are often reluctant to practice the measure of agreement we have already achieved; we remain satisfied to live in division. Therefore we cry to you, our God:

People: What has happened to us? Where did we go astray?

Silence

Leader: Gracious God, have mercy upon us, forgive us our sins and transform us so that we may live united in your love; through our Saviour, Jesus Christ,

People: Amen.

Acclamation (stand)

Je - ya Je-ya Je-ya Je - ya ho

Fine **Leader**

1. Thee - ree   saam - nee
1. We   bow be - fore   you,
1. Wir   beu- gen uns,   groß
1. A   ti ve - ni - mos,

ham   haiñ   aa - tee.   1. ham   haiñ   aa - tee,
O   great   and   ho - ly   1. O   great   and   ho - ly
bist   du   und   hei - lig.   1. Du,   groß   und   hei - lig!
Dios   bue - no y   san - to   1. Dios   bue - no y   san - to

Leader

Cha - re   no   mey   haiñ   shi - sh   na - vaa - thee.
We   bow   our   heads   to   you   great   and   ho - ly.
Wir   beu - gen   uns,   du   bist   groß   und   hei - lig.
Y   te a - do - ra - mos,   Dios   bue - no y   san - to.

All   **Leader**

Shi - sha   na - va - te.   Je - ya   Je - ya   the - ri
O   great   and   ho - ly.   Low   at   your   feet   we
Du,   groß   und   hei - lig!   Tief   zu   dei - nen   Fü - ßen
Dios   bue - no y   san - to.   Nos   in - cli - na - mos

Leader

ham   haiñ   gaa - tee   Je - ya   Je - ya   the - ri
bow   in   qui - et   rev' - rence;   then   sing   your   prais - es,
na - hen   wir   mit   An - dacht,   sin - gen   dir   zu   Eh - ren
fren - te a   tu   pre - sen - cia,   y   te a - la - ba - mos

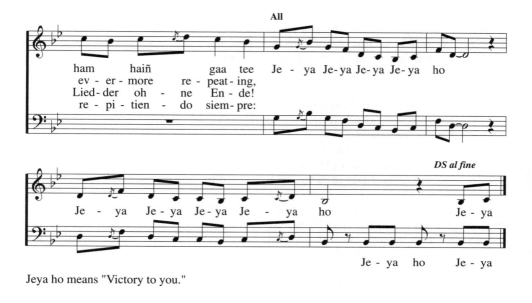

ham   haiñ   gaa   tee   Je - ya Je-ya Je-ya Je-ya   ho
ev - er - more   re - peat - ing,
Lied - der   oh - ne   En - de!
re - pi - tien - do   siem - pre:

Je - ya   Je - ya   Je-ya   Je - ya   ho   Je - ya

Je - ya   ho   Je - ya

Jeya ho means "Victory to you."

2. Lord, let us see you, grant us a vision,
(grant us a vision).
Sins and denials, dear Lord, forgive us,
(dear Lord, forgive us).
Take us and keep us in your
strong protection,
safe in your refuge, we will sing your praises.

2. Gott laß dich sehn, gib dich zu erkennen.
(laß dich erkennen.)
Sünden und Feigheit kannst du vergeben.
(du kannst vergeben.)
Nimm uns und beschütze uns mit
starken Armen,
daß bei dir geborgen wir dein Loblied singen!

New Testament Reading: Galatians 3:1-29 (sit)

Sermon (sit)

Silence (sit)

Affirmation (stand)

Leader: Sisters and brothers, in your baptism you renounced the powers of evil and confessed your allegiance to Christ. Let us now affirm our faith together.
Brothers and sisters, do you believe in God the Father?

People: We believe in God, the Father almighty,
Creator of heaven and earth.

Leader: Sisters and brothers, do you believe in Jesus Christ?
People: We believe in Jesus Christ, his only Son, our Lord.
He was conceived by the power of the Holy Spirit
and born of the virgin Mary.
He suffered under Pontius Pilate,
was crucified, died, and was buried.
He descended into hell.
On the third day he rose again.
He ascended into heaven,
and is seated at the right hand of the Father.
He will come again to judge the living and the dead.

Leader: Brothers and sisters, do you believe in the Holy Spirit?
People: We believe in the Holy Spirit,
the holy catholic church,
the communion of saints,
the forgiveness of sins,
the resurrection of the body,
and the life everlasting. Amen.

Leader: We affirm and celebrate together through the gift of Jesus Christ, that we and
our churches are in a real though still imperfect communion. We affirm and
celebrate the increasing mutual recognition of one another's baptism as the one
baptism into Christ. We will dare to explore all the ways, known and unknown,
to become one in Christ Jesus. We will not give up even in the face of
difficulties.

As baptized Christians clothed with Christ, let us claim each other as sisters
and brothers in Christ, joint heirs of the promise.

(The peace is exchanged while the choir sings)

*(At this point the leaders should greet each other in ways meaningful for the variety of
cultures. Then the members of the congregation follow suit)*

Hymn (sung by the choir)

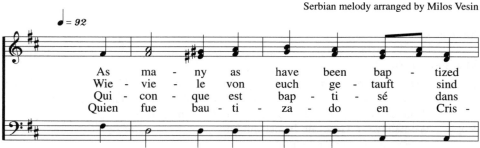

Serbian melody arranged by Milos Vesin

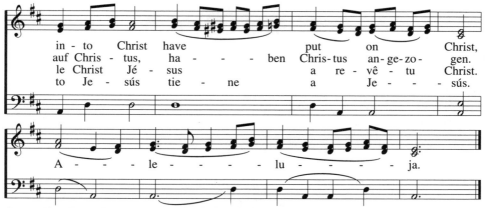

in - to Christ have ... put on Christ,
auf Chris - tus, ha - - - ben Chris- tus an - ge- zo - gen.
le Christ Jé - sus a re - vê - tu Christ.
to Je - sús tie - ne a Je - - - sús.

A - - - le - - - - lu - - - - ja.

German, Dieter Trautwein © Strube Verlag GmbH, Pettenkoferstr. 25, D-80336 München, Germany.
French, Robert Faerber © 1993 WCC. Spanish, Juan A. Gattinoni © 1993 WCC.

Prayer of Thanksgiving (stand)

Leader: We give thanks to God, the holy and undivided Trinity, that we are one in our Lord Jesus Christ, not by the agreement of our minds or the consent of our wills, but by that which he, in his unmerited grace, has done for us in his incarnation, death and resurrection, and by the gift of the Holy Spirit.

People: We thank you, O God.

Leader: We give thanks that God has called us into faith, and laid upon us an allegiance that is above all other loyalties.

People: We thank you, O God.

Leader: We give thanks for the knowledge that though we are divided in outward form, we all are the objects of the love and grace of God.

People: We thank you, O God.

Leader: We give thanks for God's gift of baptism by water and the Spirit and for the increasing recognition that this is a common sign of our communion together.

People: We thank you, O God.

Lord's Prayer (stand)

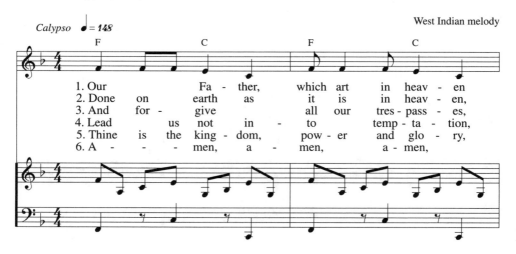

Calypso ♩ = 148   West Indian melody

1. Our   Fa - ther,   which art   in   heav - en
2. Done   on   earth   as   it   is   in   heav - en,
3. And   for - give   all   our   tres - pass - es,
4. Lead   us   not   in - to   temp - ta - tion,
5. Thine   is   the   king - dom,   pow - er   and   glo - ry,
6. A - - - men,   a - men,   a - men,

Benediction (stand)

Leader: Let us join hands and say together the grace in our own languages.

Hymn

Léonidas Ntibimenya: Rwanda

2. Munezero mu bahungu
3. Munezero mu bako bwa
4. Munezero mu basaza
5. Munezero mu banamwesa
6. Munezero mu mw'isi yose

2. Joyfully sing out all
   you young men.
3. Joyfully sing out all
   you women.
4. Joyfully sing out
   older persons.
5. Joyfully sing out all
   you children.
6. Joyfully sing out all
   you nations.

2. Chantez la joie vous
   les jeunes.
3. Chantez la joie vous
   les femmes.
4. Chantez la joie vous
   les vieux.
5. Chantez la joie vous
   les enfants.
6. Chantez la joie vous
   les nations.

When the leader points to the group mentioned in the verse, they sing louder.

3. Services for Liturgical Seasons

The theme of the WCC's seventh assembly in Canberra 1991 was "Come, Holy Spirit —
Renew the Whole Creation". One of the services therefore related to the Pentecost story.
In addition, the assembly took place at the beginning of Lent, so it was necessary to hold
an Ash Wednesday service as well. It was a quick liturgical journey in a few short days.
The following services are included as alternative ways to celebrate Ash Wednesday and
Pentecost. Services on other themes coming from the assembly are included in a later
section.

More than any other place, the huge worship tent became the central and uniting spot
of the assembly. Already at seven o'clock each morning people came to get the best seats,
despite the fact that worship did not begin until a quarter to eight.

The worship life in Canberra highlighted the need of Christians today for common
prayer and common spiritual growth; the multi-cultural, multi-confessional and multi-
lingual worship made visible the very nature of the community present in Canberra. At
the same time the worship services also reminded everyone of the deep tensions existing
within the ecumenical movement (confrontation of several theological and liturgical
traditions, efforts to express the good news through radically different cultural expressions and forms, tremendous variety of personal existential and spiritual needs and
approaches). They also succeeded in reflecting a real spirit of community because they
addressed not only the official participants (delegates, advisers and staff), but also visitors
and, above all, the local people. They helped Australian Christians to feel an integral part
of the ecumenical gathering. An important sign of this integration was the choir: about
seventy persons from Canberra, representing different congregations and various denominational backgrounds (a good number were in fact Catholic) led the congregational
singing at all morning worship services. Canberra was the direct descendant of the
worship style that had come to fruition in Vancouver.

Holy Spirit — Change Our Hearts

*This is a modification of an Ash Wednesday ritual. It has been shortened and broadened
by the use of music from many regions. It is important to observe the silences; also, the
intercessions might need to be expanded.*

*In Canberra, bowls containing ashes were brought in the Bible procession by people
dressed in sackcloth. After the blessing of the ashes, the bowls were taken to the different
exits, where people were invited to have the sign of the cross made on their foreheads.
The kyries are sung by the choir while this is taking place.*

*This would be a good foundation service for those confessions who have never used a
service of ashes. It is important that the participatory action takes place at an exit; but an
alternative exit should be available for those who do not wish to receive the ashes. In a
local congregation which has never experienced this, it would be important to preach on
it so that it is interpreted to the members. Traditionally the ashes are made by burning the*

palms from the previous year's Palm Sunday. In areas where palms are not available, other plants may be suitable. Some traditions mix the ashes with a small amount of oil but be careful with this as it can turn into a gritty lump. The darker portion of the ash works well for making the sign of the cross on the forehead.

This service is not intended to replace traditional Ash Wednesday services, although it can provide musical resources for these. It is included here as a way of sharing traditions.

* * *

Trumpet (or chofa)

Call to Worship (stand)

Leader: Blow the trumpet in Zion; sanctify a fast;
 call a solemn assembly; gather the people.
 Sanctify the congregation; assemble the aged;
 gather the children, even infants at the breast.
 Let the bridegroom leave his room,
 and the bride her canopy.

Hymn

Psalm 137:1   Anonymous

German, Wolfgang Leyk. French, Joëlle Gouël © 1990 WCC. Spanish, Federico J. Pagura © 1990 WCC.

Prayer

Leader: Let us pray:
Almighty and everlasting God,
grant through the inspiration of your Holy Spirit
that we may truly repent and change our ways.
Spare us with your forgiveness
so that we may return to your grace;
through Jesus Christ our Lord,

People: Amen.

Entrance of the Word *(sung a cappella)*

John 1:29   Rolf Schweizer: Germany

© Verlag Ernst Kaufmann, Alleestr. 2, Postfach 2208, 77993 Lahr, Germany.

Old Testament Reading: Joel 2:12-14,17-19 (sit)

Response: Siehe, das ist Gottes Lamm (stand)

Gospel Reading: Mark 1:12 and 13

Response: Siehe, das ist Gottes Lamm (stand)

Silence for Reflection (sit)

Call to Confession

Leader: Brothers and Sisters:
The use of ashes is an ancient custom of penitence which is practised
by many present-day traditions as a sign of mortality and repentance.
Ash Wednesday provides a time for us to realize that we are not
God but have been created by God from the dust of the earth and
that we will return to dust.

Silence

Confession of Sins

Leader: Let us confess our sin in the presence of God
and of one another.
Holy and Gracious God,

People: I confess that I have sinned against you.
Some of my sins, I know
— the thoughts and words and deeds of which I am ashamed —
but some are known only to you.
In the name of Jesus Christ I ask forgiveness.
Deliver and restore me, that I may be in peace.

Response: *(slow samba, rhythm instruments)*

Music, Portuguese and Spanish © Jaci Maraschin, Rua Leão XIII n 230, ap. 11, Rudge Ramos, São Bernardo do Campo 09735-220 São Paulo – SP, Brazil. French, Joëlle Gouël © 1990 WCC.

Intercession

Leader: God, our Creator,
we rejoice that you have made us
to reflect your image and to care for your creation.
Give us courage to face our failure
and limitations, and to overcome our helplessness.

Blessing of the Ashes

Leader: Lord, bless these ashes that they may become for us who bear them
a sign of our sorrow for our sins and a visible reminder
of the hope that we have in Jesus Christ your Son, our Lord.

People: Amen.

Response *(with organ)*

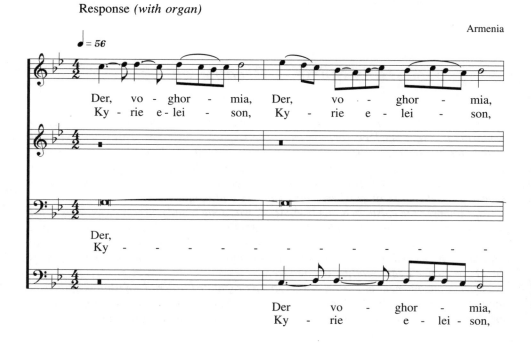

Der, vo - ghor - mia,   Der, vo - ghor - mia.
Ky - rie e - lei - son,   Ky - rie e - lei - son.

Der vo - ghor - mia.
Ky - rie e-lei - son,

rie

Der vo - ghor - mia,
Ky - rie e - lei - son,

Der vo - ghor - mia,   Der vo - ghor - mia,
Ky - rie e - lei - son,   Ky - rie e - lei - son,

Imposition of Ashes

Leader: I invite you, as you leave,
to receive on your head ashes in the sign of the cross,
the symbol of our salvation.
In the name of Jesus Christ, go in peace.

Response: Senhor, tempiedade de nós (see p.107) *(sung while leaving)*

Holy Spirit — Breathe on Us

The first Pentecost experience was in a multi-cultural and multi-lingual setting, in a context that is very much mirrored in many contemporary big cities. This worship invites us to enter into the experience of Pentecost. As we invite the Holy Spirit to breathe on us, we too overcome the confusion of languages and other differences which divide us. We discover once again the prophetic hope of Pentecost. This worship is consequently especially useful in settings where many cultures and languages meet.

In Canberra the epistle reading from Acts 2 was done in the following way: Acts 2:1-4 was read in English by one reader. Suddenly 35-40 people stood up in the congregation and read, at the same time, each one in their own language verses 5-13. The pentecostal experience happened right in the middle of the congregation! The concluding part, verses 14-21, was once again read by one reader.

During one moment in this otherwise strictly regulated order of worship people were invited to share what the Spirit might be giving to them: a song, a word of praise, and so on. In some traditions in the Christian world (especially within charismatic circles) this kind of congregational participation is common. To other traditions it might be unusual. This is the fascination about ecumenical worship: we are invited to share, test and experience each other's traditions with open hearts, minds and spirits.

A personal memory. On this particular morning God's Spirit obviously was in a good mood at the assembly; the wind of the Spirit literally breathed through the big tent. It was a gusty morning and the text from Acts 2 speaking of "the rush of a violent wind" was strongly illustrated by the powers of nature. At the moment when people were invited to share what the Spirit was speaking to them, the "dove" suddenly appeared in the tent. It circled over the crowd of three thousand people, made a spectacular loop and flew out! A slight murmur went through the congregation. Afterwards a black American delegate came up to one of the members of the worship committee and said: "How did you do that? What a fantastic illustration of the presence of the Spirit! And you folks in the worship committee seem to think of every important aspect in each detail; the dove was even black and white!" Actually, the "dove" was a very local and very lost Australian magpie, but who could tell?

In a local service it should be possible to find three, four or five people who can read in other languages. This is enough to make the experience work. Think of exchange students, those studying other languages, immigrant groups, etc.

* * *

Invocation (sit)

Leader: O, come quickly Holy Spirit,
so that we may understand your holy word.
Come, we pray, unite our hearts.
Come, we pray, increase our faith.
O, come quickly Holy Spirit.

Opening Prayer

Leader: In faith
let us come before the Holy God
and know who we are:

Silence for Personal Reflection

Response: Kyrie eleison (see p.51) *(sung a cappella)*

Leader: Holy Spirit, Holy Advocate and Comforter,
In you we celebrate the liberating
presence of the living Christ
You blow where you will,
refreshing, renewing and inspiring;
Like fire you purify.

Holy Spirit, Advocate and Comforter,
You expose what is evil in the world.
You convict the world of sin;
Like fire you purify.

Purify us, carry us beyond our
narrow personal concerns;
Uphold, preserve and care for your creation,
Nourish, sustain and direct your creatures.
Holy Spirit, Advocate and Comforter,
Like fire you purify.
Purify us, we pray.

Entrance of the Word

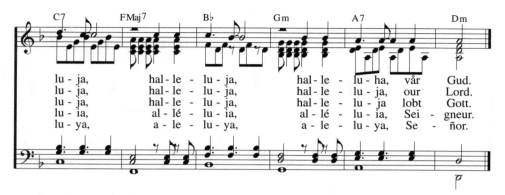

lu - ja,	hal - le - lu - ja,	hal - le - lu - ha,	vår	Gud.
lu - ja,	hal - le - lu - ja,	hal - le - lu - ja,	our	Lord.
lu - ja,	hal - le - lu - ja,	hal - le - lu - ja	lobt	Gott.
lu - ia,	al - lé - lu - ia,	al - lé - lu - ia,	Sei	- gneur.
lu - ya,	a - le - lu - ya,	a - le - lu - ya,	Se	- ñor.

Parts 1 and 2 can be sung at the same time. Teile 1 und 2 können gleichzeitig gesungen werden. Les deux parties peuvent se chanter en même temps. Las partes 1 y 2 se pueden cantar al mismo tiempo.

Melody, Swedish and English © Per Harling, Geijersgatan 18 B, 752 26 Uppsala, Sweden. German, Wolfgang Leyk. French, Joëlle Gouël © 1990 WCC. Spanish, Raquel Achon. Arrangement, Terry MacArthur © 1994 WCC.

Epistle Reading: Acts 2:1-21

Response *(sung a cappella)*

Christian I. Tamaela: Indonesia

♩ = 66

| Pu - ji Tu | - | han, | Pu - ji Tu | - | han, | Pu - ji Tu | - | han. |
| Hal - le - lu | - | ia, | Hal - le - lu | - | ia, | Hal - le - lu | - | ia. |

© The Asian School of Music, Worship and the Arts, P.O. Box 10533 Broadway Centrum, Quezon City 1112 Philippines.

Gospel Reading: John 21:21-23

Response: Puji Tuhan

Reflection (sit)

Leader: Sisters and brothers in Christ, Peter proclaimed on the day of Pentecost the prophetic promise: "I will pour out my Spirit on all flesh." We are the inheritors of that promise. "Come, Holy Spirit" is not just a prayer for some future manifestation. It is also the belief that the Spirit is visiting us, here and now. We are together from many nations and cultures around the world, and we are speaking about God's works of power. We are calling upon the name of the Lord. Jesus is in our midst saying to us, "Peace — receive the Holy Spirit."

(Take a moment to listen to the Spirit. In the silence the Spirit may give you a word or a song or a deeper quietness than words or song. If a word or song comes to mind, speak it aloud. Let the Spirit lead so that together we offer our prayers and praise that the Spirit is with us.)

Time of Praise

Response: Sanna, sannanina (see pp.70-71) *(sung a cappella)*

Prayers of Intercession

Leader: O God, into the pain of the tortured:
People: breathe stillness.

Leader: Into the hunger of the very poor:
People: breathe fullness.

Leader: Into the wounds of our planet:
People: breathe well-being.

Leader: Into the deaths of your creatures:
People: breathe life.

Leader: Into those who long for you:
People: breathe yourself.

Leader: Your kingdom come, your will be done.
People: The kingdom, the power and the glory
are yours now and forever.

Leader: Our God is with us.
We celebrate the miracle of living and being!
We celebrate the miracle of creation!
People: Our God loves us,
our lives are the blessing of God,
let us give thanks with joy!
Amen.

Lord's Prayer (in your own language)

Benediction (stand)

Leader: God of power,
may the boldness of your Spirit transform us,
may the gentleness of your Spirit lead us,
may the gifts of your Spirit
equip us and send us forth into the world
with a passion for service.
Through Jesus Christ our Lord,
People: Amen.

Song: You are holy (see pp.112-114)

4. Services on Justice, Peace and the Integrity of Creation

One of the priorities of the World Council of Churches is work on justice, peace and the integrity of creation. These themes were the source for some of the worship services at the Canberra assembly.

Giver of Life — Sustain Your Creation

This worship focused on our responsibility for creation. The hymn "God made the crystal clear waters" helped visualize this. The verses were sung by soloists and everyone joined in the refrain. During the first four verses people carrying baskets of fruit and vegetables, flowers, clean water, put them under and around the altar and the presenters moved slowly around the altar. After a moment of silence verses 5 and 6 were sung during which the presenters put a thin black cloth over the fruits of creation and knelt in a position of "despair" during the confession of sins. Another option would be to bring in rubbish, for example, paper cups, dirty water, old boxes, cans, etc., and put them on top of the fruits of creation. As words of forgiveness verses 7-9 were sung and the Bible was brought in a procession. The black cloth was taken away (or the rubbish is taken away) and some of the fruits were put on the altar as an offering of thankfulness.

* * *

Invocation

I-to Loh: Taiwan

> Giv - er of life, sus - tain Your cre - a - tion.
> Du Le - bens - grund, be - schüt–ze dei - ne Schöp - fung.
> Ô Dieu de vie, sou - tiens ta cré - a - tion.
> Oh Cre - a - dor, sos - tén tu cre - a - ción.

Call to Worship

Leader 1:   Glory to you, Almighty God.
             You spoke, and light came out of darkness,
             order rose from confusion.

Leader 2:   Glory to you, Jesus Christ!
You met us as a refugee, a threatened child,
the word made flesh, born in a forgotten place.

Leader 3:   Glory to you, Holy Spirit!
You brooded over chaos,
mothering and shaping God's new creation.

Leader 4:   Glory to you, God, Three-in-One!
You are surrounded by the song of the saints in heaven
and you are present with us now.

Hymn: (verses 1-4) (stand)

Olov. Hartman: Sweden   Bertil Hallin: Sweden

♩ = 84 **Leader**

Gud   ska - pa - de   de   kla - ra   vatt - nen   och   tän - de
God   made   the   crys - tal   clear   wa - ters   and   there   was
L'eau   viv',   et   la   pluie   sur   les   champs   qui   tom - be   au
Dios   hi - zo al   a - gua   cris - ta - li - na,   la   tie - rra

liv   med   de - ras   sy - re,   och   vin - dar   blås - te   ö - ver
land   for   rain   to   fall on.   The   Spir - it   moved   up - on   the
prin - temps.   Dieu   les   cré - a,   Son   Es - prit   se   mou - vait   sur
don - de   cae   la   llu - via.   Su   Es - pí - ri - tu   so - bre   los

Refrain All

ha - vet.   Gud   såg   att   det   var   gott.   Gud   såg   att   det   var
o - cean.   God   saw   that   it   was   good.   God   saw   that   it   was
l'on - de,   Dieu   vit   que   c'é - tait   bon.   Dieu   vit   que   c'é - tait
ma - res.   Dios   vio   que   e - ra   bueno.   Dios   vio   que   e - ra

gott.   Och   det   vart   af - ton   och   det   vart   mor - gon.
good,   And   there was   eve - ning and   there was   morn - ing.
bon.   Et   il   y   eut un   soir et   un   ma - tin.
bueno,   y   fue   la   no - che   y   la   ma - ña - na.

Melody © Bertil Hallin, Nicoloviusgatan 8B4tr, S-217 57 Malmö, Sweden Text © Olov Hartman, Sweden 1970, Estate of Rev. Olov Hartman, c/o Per Hartman, Grevgat. 14, S-64330 Vingåker, Sweden. English, Maria Klasson Sundin, adapt. Per Harling. French, Joëlle Gouël © 1990 WCC. Spanish, vs. 1-4 Pablo Sosa, vs. 5-9 Jorge Maldonado © 1990 WCC.

2. Gud vävde gräsets gröna matta
med starr och hundkäx och violer
i väldiga och skira mönster.
Gud såg att det var gott.

3. Och havet vimlade av fiskar
och luften vimlade av fåglar
och se, vad fjärilar på ängen!
Gud såg att det var gott.

4. Ett ord, ett öga--allting föddes
i människan till namn och tanke
och talade med Gud på jorden.
Gud såg att det var gott.

2. God wove the tapestry of green grass,
embroided flowers, bees and mushrooms,
and fashioned trees within the garden.
God saw that it was good.

3. God made the fish and life of oceans
and all the birds that fly above us.
On land there were all kinds of creatures.
God saw that it was good.

4. A man, a woman in God's image,
in full communion with creation,
were loving, sharing with each other.
God saw that it was good.

2. Tissage vert, herbe des prés,
tulip' et scarabées. Dieu les créa.
Dans le jardin, mit le grand chêne,
Dieu vit que c'était bon.

3. Des poissons tout plein les étangs,
merles et papillons, Dieu les créa.
Des bêtes partout sur la terre,
Dieu vit que c'était bon.

4. A son image Dieu les fit,
homme, femme, pleine communion,
aimant et partageant ensemble,
Dieu vit que c'était bon.

2. Tejió después verdes alfombras,
bordó las flores y los frutos,
los árboles plantó en su huerto.
Dios vio que era bueno.

3. Les dio los peces a los mares
y al cielo regaló las aves.
Llenó la tierra de animales.
Dios vio que era bueno.

4. La humanidad creó a su imagen,
mujer y hombre en comunión
su amor comparten, sus cuidados.
Dios vio que era bueno.

Silence

Confession of Sins: God made the crystal (verses 5-6) (sit)

5. Men fåglar dör och gräset vissnar
och vattnet grumlas i var källa
där människan går fram på jorden.
Gud såg att det var ont.
Gud såg att det var ont.
Och det vart afton och det vart morgon.

6. Det gamla skapelseförbundet
med jord och himmel ligger brutet--
en ovän kom och gjorde detta.
Gud såg att det var ont.

5. But birds are dying, grass is withering
and poisoned waters kill our children.
The paradise is lost for profit.
God saw the goodness lost.
God saw the goodness lost
and there was evening and there was morning.

6. The covenant of all creation
between the earth and heav'n is broken.
The earth is ruled by hate and evil.
God saw the goodness lost.

5. Soudain, le jardin se ferma.
Royaumes et rivaux dominèrent.
Des tours, des murs, les rois bâtirent,
Dieu ne vit plus le bien.
Dieu ne vit plus le bien.
Et il y eut un soir et un matin.

6. Toute la création languit,
l'eau est souillée, nos petits se meurent.
Toute notre puissance tombe,
Dieu ne vit plus le bien.

5. La creación, los niños mueren,
contaminados son los mares,
el paraíso se ha estropeado.
Lo bueno se acabó.
Lo bueno se acabó.
y fue la noche y la mañana.

6. El pacto hecho entre lo eterno
y lo terreno ahora es roto.
El mal gobierna en todas partes.
Lo bueno se acabó.
Lo bueno se acabó. . .

Leader: Giver of Life,
In the midst of a plundered earth we groan with creation:
People: Have mercy on us.

Leader: Giver of Life,
In the midst of poisoned waters we groan with creation:
People: Have mercy on us.

Leader: Giver of Life,
In the midst of polluted air we groan with creation:
People: Have mercy on us.

Leader: Giver of Life,
In the midst of mountains of waste we groan with creation:
People: Have mercy on us.

Leader: Giver of life,
In the midst of a world at war we groan with creation:
People: Have mercy on us.

Leader: Giver of Life,
           we who are made in the image of God have gone astray,
           and creation groans with us:
People: Have mercy on us.

Silence

Entrance of the Word: God made the crystal (verses 7-9) (stand)

7. När Jesus gick omkring ibland oss
och gjorde väl och hjälpte alla
förstod vi hur det var från början.
Gud såg att det var gott.
Gud såg att det var gott.
Och det vart afton och det vart morgon.

8. En reningseld är tänd i världen,
ett nytt förbund med jord och himmel
är stiftat i ett bröd som brytes.
Gud såg att det var gott.

9. Gud skapar allt på nytt i Kristus
som älskar syndaren och sparven
och ger en öppen rymd åt båda.
Gud såg att det var gott.

7. When Jesus walked his way among us
we were reminded of God's image
and how it was from the beginning.
God saw that it was good.
God saw that it was good.
and there was evening and there was
morning.

8. The Spirit's fire burns within us
to care again for all creation
in covenant of bread that's broken.
God saw that it was good.

9. All things will be renewed in Jesus,
who loves both sinners and creation.
Our future will be life forever.
God saw that it was good.

7. Quand Jésus parmi nous descendit
image réelle du Dieu vivant,
commencement de nos mémoires.
Dieu vit que c'était bon.
Dieu vit que c'était bon.
Et il y eut un soir et un matin.

8. Le feu de l'Esprit nous invite
à prendre soin de la création,
à rompre le pain de l'alliance.
Dieu vit que c'était bon.

9. Voici toute chose est nouvelle
pour le pécheur, pour la création.
En Christ est la vie éternelle.
Dieu vit que c'était bon.

7. Cuando Jesús entró en la historia,
nos recordó de nuestro orígen:
creados por Dios, a su imágen.
Dios vio que era bueno.

8. Cuando el Espíritu nos toca
volvemos a cuidar la tierra
en conpromiso y esperanza.
Dios vio que era bueno.

9. En Jesucristo se renueva
la creación, la humanidad, la vida.
Ya disfrutamos de futuro.
Dios vio que era bueno.

Old Testament Reading: Deuteronomy 30:15-20

Response (stand)

New Testament Reading: Revelations 22:1-3

Response: Gloria, gloria, gloria

Affirmation of Faith

Leader: O God, the source of our being
        and the goal of all our longing
        we believe and trust in you.
        The whole earth is alive with your glory,
        and all that has life is sustained by you.
        We commit ourselves to cherish your world,
        and seek your face.

People: O God, embodied in a human life,
        we believe and trust in you.

Leader: Jesus, our brother, born of the woman Mary,
you confronted the proud and the powerful,
and welcomed as your friends those of no account.
Holy wisdom of God, firstborn of creation,
you emptied yourself of power
and became foolishness for our sake.
You laboured with us upon the cross,
and have brought us forth
to the hope of resurrection.
We commit ourselves to struggle against evil
and to choose life.

People: O God, life-giving Spirit,
Spirit of healing and comfort,
of integrity and truth,
we believe and trust in you.

Leader: Warm-winged Spirit, brooding over creation,
rushing wind and Pentecostal fire,
we commit ourselves to work with you
and renew our world.

Intercession (sit)

Leader: Spirit of God, intercede for us,
Give voice to the weeping of the world,
Name for us the pain of your creation.
Spirit of God, intercede for us now.

Response: Giver of life, sustain your creation (see p.116) *(sung a cappella; if there is a gong it can be used on the last note)*

Leader: Spirit of God,
come search our hearts.
Bring to life the seeds of hope.
Point us sharply to truths that we know.
Spirit of God, come search our hearts now.

Response: Giver of life, sustain your creation.

Leader: Spirit of God, open us to your will.
Gather around us your goodness.
Take the things which we have destroyed,
Take the brokenness of our living
and renew the whole creation with your saving grace.

Response: Giver of life, sustain your creation.

Lord's Prayer (in your own language)

Leader: Sisters and brothers, God has formed us from the dust of the earth, and has breathed into us the spirit of life. This spirit calls us to join in the holy act of creation and preservation of all that God has made.

This gracious invitation confronts us with choices. We have set before us this day choices of life and of death. When we pray, "Giver of life, sustain your creation", we commit ourselves to choosing life, for the healing of the nations and for the care and redemption of all that God has made.

Let us join together to affirm our choice for life, and our commitment to cherish God's world and to work to sustain all of creation.

Blessing

Leader: Eternal God, our beginning and our end,
be our starting point and our heaven
and accompany us in this day's journey.
Use our hands to do the work of your creation
and use our lives to bring others the new life you give this world
in Jesus Christ, Redeemer of all.
People: Amen.

Hymn *(sung with drums)*

as taught by Daisy Nshakazongwe: Botswana

$\flat = 162$

Re - a - mo le - bo - ga, re - a - mo le - bo - ga,
We give our thanks to Him, we give our thanks to Him,
Wir dan - ken un - serm Gott, wir dan - ken un - serm Gott,
Mer - ci à Toi Sei - gneur, mer - ci à Toi Sei - gneur,

re - a - mo le - bo - ga mo - di - mo wa ro - na.
we give our thanks to Him, we give thanks to our God.
wir dan - ken un - serm Gott, der Dank gilt un - serm Gott.
mer - ci à Toi Sei - gneur, nous te ren - dons grâ - ce.

(Variation in stz. 2, 3)

2. Ga a yo yo tshwa-nang le - we - na
3. Re - pho - lo si - tswe ke - we - na

2. There is no one
   like Him. (3x)
There's no one like our God.

3. We have been saved
   by Him. (3x)
We've been saved by our
God.

2. Denn Gott ist
   niemand gleich. (3x)
niemand gleicht unserm Gott.

3. Wir sind durch
   Gott befreit. (3x)
befreit durch unsern Gott.

2. Aucun n'est comme Toi. (3x)
Comme Toi, Oh Seigneur.

3. C'est lui qui nous sauva. (3x)
C'est Dieu qui nous sauva.

Transcribed and English paraphrase by I-to Loh © 1986 WCC and The Asian School of Music, Worship and the Arts.
German, Wolfgang Leyk. French, Joëlle Gouël © 1990 WCC.

Spirit of Truth — Set Us Free

This service at Canberra focused on bondage and different kinds of lack of freedom. For the lament we had four groups of people in the four corners of the worship tent. The people in each group carried a large chain as a symbol of bondage. After each leader's lamentation one of the groups shouted, "This is not right, Lord." The congregation responded with the same words. The chains were then shaken. During the singing of "Oh, freedom" the four groups moved to the altar area, still "bound" to one another by the chain, and circled the altar with their chains. At the end of the song the Bible was brought in. During the whole service the groups, bound together by the chains and surrounding the altar, were in full view of the congregation. During the prayers of intercession the chains were held high. After the Lord's prayer the chains were dropped on the floor as a sound of freedom.

* * *

Call to Worship (stand)

Leader: Sisters and brothers
          we have come together
          to worship God who offers us freedom
          through our Lord Jesus Christ.
          For the Spirit of life in Christ Jesus
          has set us free from the law of sin and death.
          For we did not receive a spirit of slavery
          to fall back into fear
          but we have received the spirit
          of the children of God.

Hymn

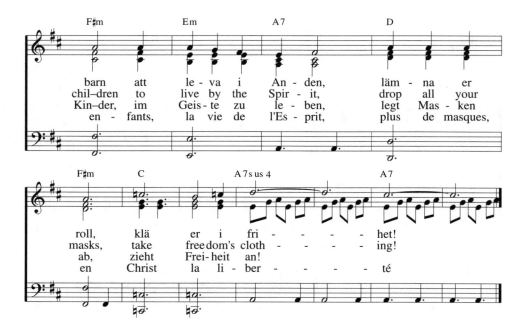

barn att le - va i An - den, läm - na er
chil–dren to live by the Spir - it, drop all your
Kin–der, im Geis - te zu le - ben, legt Mas - ken
en - fants, la vie de l'Es - prit, plus de masques,

roll, klä er i fri - - - - het!
masks, take free dom's cloth - - - - ing!
ab, zieht Frei- heit an!
en Christ la li - ber - - - - té

2. Himmel på jorden,
här får vi leva,
älska och ge,
burna av glädje.
Öva er barn
att leva i Anden,
våga idag
smaka Guds framtid.

2. Kingdom of God,
present among us,
gives to us all
strength for the journey.
Practise my children
to live by the Spirit,
tasting today
hope of God's future!

2. Himmel auf Erden,
hier wo wir wohnen,
teilen die Gaben,
freudig gebracht.
Lernt meine Kinder
im Geiste zu leben
spürt heute schon,
Hoffnung und Zukunft.

3. Såren kan läkas,
maskerna faller,
mänska av Gud,
avspeglar Kristus.
Öva er barn
att leva i Anden,
himlen är här,
evig i tiden.

3. Wounds will be healed,
eyes will be opened,
imaging God,
reflecting Jesus,
practice my children
to live by the Spirit,
heaven is here,
time made eternal!

3. Wunden verheilen,
wir sehen plötzlich
Gottes Gesicht
in Jesus an.
Lernt meine Kinder
im Geiste zu leben
Himmel ist hier,
Zeit dauert ewig.

2. Le ciel a visité notre terre,
Partage et joie
De tous les dons.
Vivez, mes enfants, la vie de l'Esprit,
Goûtez l'espoir, en Christ
est l'avenir.

3. Toutes nos plaies et nos meurtrissures
Nos yeux verront
la guérison.
Vivez, mes enfants, la vie de l'Esprit,
Car ici-bas commence,
l'éternité.

Lament (sit)

Leader: It is not right, Lord,
        that though there is enough land, people still are landless.
Voice: This is not right, Lord.
People: This is not right, Lord.

(Chains are shaken)

Leader: It is not right, Lord,
        that though there is enough land, people still are starving.
Voice: This is not right, Lord.
People: This is not right, Lord.

(Chains are shaken)

Leader: It is not right, Lord,
        that though you have made all human beings equal,
        people are still prejudiced because of race, faith or ideology.
Voice: This is not right, Lord.
People: This is not right, Lord.

(Chains are shaken)

Leader: It is not right, Lord,
        that though you have given us bodies, which are temples of your Holy Spirit,
        people still are captive to drugs and other means of abuse.
Voice: This is not right, Lord.
People: This is not right, Lord.

(Chains are shaken)

Entrance of the Word (stand)

African American traditional

bur-ied in my grave, An' go home to my Lord an' be free.
bur-ied in my grave, An' go home to my Lord an' be free.

3. No mo' weepin'

4. There'll be singin'

5. There'll be shoutin'

6. There'll be prayin'

Old Testament Reading: Jeremiah 34:12-17 (sit)

Response: Puji Tuhan (see p.114) *(sung a cappella and in unison; a gong can be used on the last note)*

Gospel Reading: John 8:31-36

Response: Puji Tuhan

Affirmation of Faith

Leader: We believe in God,
Women: Whose breath gives energy for the struggle,
Men: Whose power goes beyond human weakness.

Leader: We believe in Christ,
Women: Whose solidarity accompanies all our deaths.
Men: Whose life frees us to the resurrection.

Leader: We believe in the Spirit,
Women: Who liberates us from powerlessness
Men: and brings us towards all truth.

Leader: We believe in God the Holy Trinity,
People: Whose grace upholds our being,
              whose unity calls us to be the church
              and to live out the hope of the kingdom.

Intercessions (sit)

Leader: The chains are still there,
              but, in Christ, they cannot bind us.
              In the power of the Holy Spirit
              we will claim our freedom
              from the powers of sin and death.

Response *(sung a cappella)*   Dinah Reindorf: Ghana

Hal-le - lu - jah!   Hal-le - lu - jah!   Hal-le-lu - jah!

Hal-le - lu - jah!   Hal-le - lu - jah!   Hal - le-lu - jah!

© Dinah Reindorf, P.O. Box 13060, Accra, Ghana.

Leader: We claim freedom for all people who live
         under oppressive systems.
         Let us name those places...

         Silence

Leader: Come, Holy Spirit, and set us free.

         Response: Hallelujah

Leader: We claim freedom for the earth itself,
         that it will be released from exploitation and pollution,
         from destruction and war.
         Come, Holy Spirit, and set us free.

         Response: Hallelujah

Leader: We claim freedom for the churches
         that we will find new ways towards unity
         and live in faithfulness to the gospel.
         Come, Holy Spirit, and set us free.

         Response: Hallelujah

Leader: We claim freedom for ourselves
         from all the things that bind us
         — our fear, our lack of worth,
         our pride and our unbelief.
         Come, Holy Spirit, and set us free.

         Response: Hallelujah

Lord's Prayer (in your own language)

Benediction (stand)

Leader: May the grace of God enfold us,
         the love of Christ uphold us
         and the Spirit of truth set us free.
         Go forward in faith,
         transform the chains that bind the world
         to a chain of solidarity.

Hymn *(sung a cappella)*

South Africa

♩ = 120

Siph' a - man - dla Nko - si. Wo-kung-e - sa - bi. Siph'
O God give us pow - er to rip down pri - sons. O
O Gott gib uns Stär - ke, dass Ket - ten sprin- gen. O
O Sei- gneur, don - ne- nous ta puis- san - ce pour
Di - os, da - nos fuer - za bo - tar pri - sio - nes. Di -

a - man - dla Nko - si. Si - ya - wa - ding - a.
God give us pow - er to lift the peo - ple.
Gott, gib uns Stär - ke, dass wir auf - ste - hen.
dé - truire les pri - sons ai - der les peu - ples.
os da - nos fuer - za al - zar al pueb - lo.

2. O God give us courage
to withstand hatred.
O God give us courage
not to be bitter.

2. O Gott gib uns Hoffnung
Dem Hass zu wehren
O Gott gib uns Hoffnung
Nicht zu verbittern.

2. O Seigneur, donne-nous
ton courage
pour vaincre la haine
et l'amertume.

3. O God give us power
and make us fearless.
O God give us power
because we need it.

3. O Gott gib uns Stärke
Und mach uns furchtlos
O Gott gib uns Stärke
Weil wir sie brauchen.

3. O Seigneur, donne-nous
ta puissance
pour être sans faiblesse
Viens-nous en aide.

2. Dios, danos fuerza andar sin miedo.
Dios, danos fuerza te lo pedimos.

Holy Spirit — Challenge Us

The basic action of this service is one of affirming the treasure God has given through our Christian sisters and brothers. In informal settings people might be encouraged to name aloud those in whom they have experienced God working. In larger more formal settings small pieces of paper could be used and then collected in clay pots. The affirmations could then be taken up by the ministers as part of a prayer of thanksgiving or printed in the church newsletter. In very large settings the example of the assembly could be followed.

In Canberra everyone was given a card with a picture of a potter. In a local setting one might ask a Sunday school class to draw a picture of a potter or of a clay pot. After the gospel reading people were invited to write down "treasures which have challenged you at this assembly and promises to reshape your life or the life of the church". Afterwards people offered these cards to each other "as a reminder of how the Spirit challenges us".

* * *

Invocation (stand)

Leader: O that you would tear open the
heavens and come down
so that the mountains would quake
at your presence —

Bow your heavens, O Lord, and come down.

Breathe into our bones a fresh
wind from the North and the South,
from the East and the West.
Give us a new flesh, a new spirit, a new heart.

Response *(sung with drums or rattles)*

Caroline Rockson: Ghana

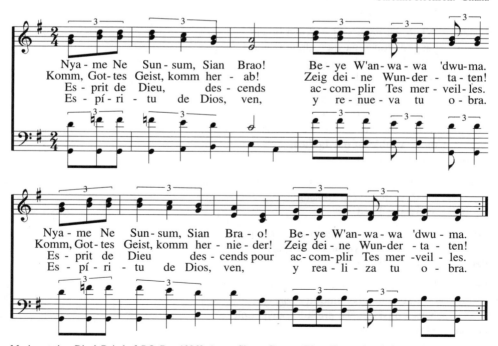

Music notation, Dinah Reindorf, P.O. Box 13060, Accra, Ghana, German, Dieter Trautwein, © Strube Verlag GmbH, Pettenkoferstr. 24, D-80336 München, Germany. French, Joëlle Gouël © 1990 WCC. Spanish, Federico J. Pagura © 1990 WCC.

Leader: Challenge us, renew us and claim us
          until we become refashioned as your people
          in the name of the Blessed Trinity
          — One God in three persons.
People: Amen.

Prayer of Confession (sit)

Leader: When we have afflicted others
          whether by our own power
          or by our silent support of systems
          which oppress, enslave and crush,
People: Break us, Lord.

Leader: When we have perplexed others
          and purposely confused them for our own gain
          or driven them to despair,
People: Break us, Lord.

Leader: When we have persecuted others,
          casting them out of our community
          leaving them forsaken and alone,
People: Break us, Lord.

Leader: When we have struck down others
          casting stones on their dreams and hopes
          until they are destroyed,
People: Break us, Lord.

Leader: Then broken, we carry in our
          bodies the death of Jesus
          so that the life of Jesus may be
          made visible in our bodies.
People: Make us, Lord.

Leader: With the power which belongs only to You,
          make us into your treasure.
People: Make us, Lord.

Leader: We are the clay, and you are the potter
          We are the work of your hands.
People: Make us, Lord.

Leader: Do not be exceedingly angry and
          do not remember iniquity forever.
          Now consider, we are all your people.
People: Make us, Lord.

Silence for Confession

Leader: Through the broken body of
          Christ, we are broken.
          Through the breath of the Spirit, we are remade.
          The Spirit challenges us to live
          as the forgiven, joyful people of God.
People: Amen.

Entrance of the Word (stand): (Gloria a Dios... Peru) (see p.31) *(v.1, sung a cappella)*

Old Testament Reading: Jeremiah 18:1-6

Response (Gloria a Dios, v.2)

Epistle Reading: 2 Corinthians 4:7-10

Response (Gloria a Dios, v.3)

Gospel Reading: John 8:3-11

Silence (sit)

Leader: Sisters and brothers, the Holy Spirit is always challenging us. We are ready to
          throw stones, to destroy, or cast out, only to discover the One who silently
          writes in the earth and convicts us with "let anyone among you who is without
          sin". It is easy to throw stones and to smash each other's creations and thoughts
          in the name of our own ways and traditions. We strive to convince rather than
          understand, to speak rather than listen.
              Yet, the Spirit is at work. In our midst is much treasure in common clay
          vessels — common human beings. Their extraordinary power belongs to God.
          They are afflicted but not crushed — persecuted, forsaken, struck down, but not
          destroyed. The Spirit challenges us through them. The Spirit remakes us as our
          old assumptions are tested by their stories and lives.
              In your worship sheet is a picture of a potter. Take a moment to name one of
          the treasures which has challenged you at this assembly (or during the past days)
          and promises to reshape your life or the life of your church. In two or three
          phrases write this on the back of the picture. In this way give thanks for this
          work of the Spirit in our midst. When you have finished, offer your card to your
          neighbour to keep as a reminder of how the Spirit challenges us.

Song: Reamo leboga (see p.123) *(sung a cappella)*

Closing Prayer

Leader: Challenge us, God, to lay down our stones and embrace the afflicted, the
          persecuted and the perplexed. We thank you for the grace which opens us to
          receive all your treasures — gifts that reshape us into the image of Jesus Christ,
          your Son.
People: Amen.

Lord's Prayer (in your own language)

Benediction

Leader: Go on your way, and from now on do not sin again.
          May God, who is the great potter, make you new, and bless you,
          now and evermore.
People: Amen.

Song

5. Prayer Services

For some services, an act of prayer becomes the central focus. All worship involves prayer, but in these services prayer does not just have its appointed place in the service. The whole service leads to prayer.

"Find Self-Control"

This service was used at the Moscow central committee meeting in 1989. It was part of a series on the fruits of the Spirit and the title reflects this. The prayers are for healing. In Moscow three persons, all ordained, stood at the front of the assembly. Those who wished came forward to one of the three. The action was simple: the celebrants took the people by the hand and offered words of blessing. We did not prescribe what these words would be. We were careful not to use oil, or to have the celebrants put their hands on the people's heads. This would have been considered too sacramental to be shared across confessions. In local settings, the ancient action of anointing with oil might be used or people might kneel before the celebrant. The pastors would then pray in a specific way for each person. The element of physical touch is very important.

This would be a good introductory service in a congregation which had never experienced such a worship before. If this action is very new to people, it helps if two of the congregation are forewarned and are prepared to come forward. Be prepared for many people to come. Pastoral care should be taken very seriously. Assistants should be prepared for counselling some with difficult needs.

* * *

Opening Prayer

Leader: God's perfect law revives the soul.
          God's word makes wise the simple.
          God's clear commands rejoice the heart.
          God's light the eye enlightens.
People: Lord, who can tell the secret faults
          that have dominion over me?
          Hold back thy servant from self will
          and break its power to bind me.
          May all I think and all I say
          be now acceptable to you,
          my Rock and my Redeemer. (Ps. 19:7-14)

Song: Santo (see pp.37-38)

Collect

Leader: Almighty God, whose Son Jesus Christ
was tempted as we are, yet without sin:
give us grace to discipline ourselves in obedience to your Spirit;
and, as you know our weakness,
so may we know your power to save;
through Jesus Christ our Lord.

People: Amen.

Hymn

Bianco of Siena
Richard F. Littledale   ♩ = 60

Ralph Vaughan Williams: England

1. Come down, O Love di - vine, seek thou this soul of
2. O let it free - ly burn, till earth - ly pas - sions
3. Let ho - ly char - i - ty my out - ward ves - ture
4. And so the yearn - ing strong, with which the soul will

mine, and vis - it it with thine own ar - dour glow - ing;
turn to dust and ash - es in its heat con - sum - ing;
be, and low - li - ness be - come mine in - ner cloth - ing;
long, shall far out - pass the power of hu - man tell - ing;

O Com - fort - er, draw near, with - in my heart ap -
and let thy glo - rious light shine ev - er on my
true low - li - ness of heart, which takes the hum - bler
for none can guess its grace, till Love cre - ate a

pear, and kin - dle it, thy ho - ly flame be - stow - ing.
sight, and clothe me round, the while my path il - lum - ing.
part, and o'er its own short - com - ings weeps with loath - ing.
place where - in the Ho - ly Spir - it makes a dwell - ing.

Music © Oxford University Press, 70 Baker Street, London W1M 1DJ, UK.

Prayer of Thanksgiving and Confession

Leader: The Apostle Paul wrote:
          In my inner being I delight in God's law, but I see another law at work in the
          members of my body, waging war against the law of my mind and making me a
          prisoner of the law of sin at work within my members. Who will rescue me from
          this body of death? Thanks be to God through Jesus Christ our Lord!

People: Thanks be to God through Jesus Christ our Lord! (Rom. 7:15-18b,22-25)

Leader: O God, Giver of life, Bearer of Pain, Maker of Love,
          we thank you that,
          you are able to accept in us what we cannot even acknowledge,
          you are able to name in us what we cannot bear to speak of;
          you are able to hold in your memory what we have tried to forget;
          you are able to hold out to us the glory that we cannot conceive.
          Have mercy on us this day,
          reconcile us through your cross to all that we have rejected in ourselves,
          that we may find no part of your creation to be alien or strange to us,
          and that we ourselves may be made whole.
          Through Jesus Christ our Lord.

People: Amen.

Entrance of the Word (stand)

Russia

Al-le-lu - ja, Al-le-lu - ja,   Al-le-lu - ja!

Gospel Reading: Mark 5:1-15

Response to the Word

Leader: As with scarlet and fine linen your church is adorned with the blood of your
          martyrs in all the world, and through them she cries aloud to Thee, O Christ our
          God: have compassion on your people, grant peace to your flock, and to our
          souls great mercy.

Prayers for Healing

Leader: Jesus asked the demoniac his name — in order to understand his character, his
          essence. The reply that his name was Legion immediately explained to Jesus the
          internal state of the man's life. He had no control, he was not one, but many, all
          the driving forces within him were at war with each other.
              Jesus invites us to name the contradictions inside of us, which we cannot
          control. We stand for justice — but enjoy the fruits of injustice. We are
          concerned for the preservation of creation — but participate in its destruction.

Like the Gerasene demoniac, we recognize the conflict within ourselves towards Jesus; on the one hand rushing up to him, and on the other hand begging him to go. As the Apostle Paul testified: I do not understand what I do, for what I want to do I do not do, but what I hate, I do. For I have the desire to do what is good, but I cannot carry it out. Let us in silence before God name the contradictions inside of us.

Silence

Leader: In the ancient tradition of the church you are invited to come forward to pray for healing; the healing of your spirit and/or body, or the healing of someone else, and then to receive from one of the celebrants a blessing.

Song *(sung a cappella)*

Jacques Berthier: Taizé, France

Na - da te tur - be, na - da te es - pan - te, quien a Dios tie - ne
Noth-ing can trou-ble, noth-ing can fright-en those who seek God shall

na - da le fal - ta. Na - da te tur - be, na - da te es - pan - te, só - lo Dios bas-ta.
nev-er go want-ing. Noth-ing can trou-ble, noth-ing can fright-en, God a-lone fills us.

Nichts beunruhige dich, nichts ängstige dich: Wer Gott hat, dem fehlt nichts.
   Gott allein genügt.
Que rien ne te trouble, rien ne t'effraie: qui a Dieu ne manque de rien. Seul Dieu suffit.

Music J. Berthier © Ateliers et Presses de Taizé, 71250 Taizé, France

Benediction

Leader: May the blessing of God who risked everything for our sake,
the blessing of the Christ-child who releases in us new visions of hope,
and the blessing of the Holy Spirit who guides and directs us
into new forms of obedience, be with us all.
People: Amen.

"Come, Holy Spirit — Renew the Whole Creation"

This was the closing service for the central committee meeting in Geneva in 1990. A similar version was used at the Canberra assembly but this one is more adaptable to local situations. It is designed as an evening service which takes its form from Isaiah 6. Because of the biblical text incense is used. For some traditions this is unusual and for some people the smell is difficult. But this is also a service which demonstrates that we are able to borrow symbols from traditions not our own in order to evoke the image or message of the biblical text. We used a large bowl to carry the incense: a smaller container inside held the charcoal and the incense itself. Make sure the bowl will not break with the heat. This method helps people experience the incense without having to learn the intricacies of thuribles. If one has never used incense, this might be a good opportunity for ecumenical learning by asking a nearby Roman Catholic or Anglican for assistance with it.

* * *

African Invocation

Ntsikana's Bell

Ntsikana: Xhosa, South Africa

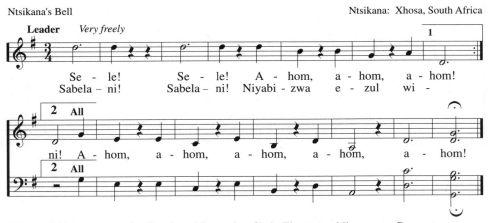

Sele and Ahom are words of praise addressed to God. The second line says: Come, come, you are called to heaven.

Words and Music © Lumko Music Department, P.O. Box 5058, 1403 Delmenville, South Africa.

Call to Worship (stand)

Leader: In mystery and grandeur
         we see the face of God.
People: In earthiness and ordinary
         we know the love of Christ.

Leader: In heights and depths
          and life and death
People: the Spirit of God is moving among us.

Leader: Let us praise God

Hymn

Kölner Gesangbuch: Germany

♩ = 84

1. From all that dwell be - low the skies let the Cre - a - tor's praise a - rise. Al-le - lu - ja. Al-le - lu - ja! Let the Re - deem - er's name be sung through eve - ry land in eve - ry
2. Thou rush - ing wind that art so strong ye clouds that sail in heaven a - long Al-le - lu - ja. Al-le - lu - ja! Thou ris - ing morn, in praise re - joice ye lights of eve - ning, find a
3. Dear mo - ther earth, who day by day un - fold - est bless-ings on our way, Al-le - lu - ja. Al-le - lu - ja! The flowers and fruits that in thee grow, let them God's glo - ry al - so
4. Let all things their Cre - a - tor bless, and wor - ship God in hum - ble - ness, Al-le - lu - ja. Al-le - lu - ja! Praise, praise the Fa - ther, praise the Son, and praise the Spir - it, Three in

Verse 1 Isaac Watts. Verses 2-4 Francis of Assisi translated by William H. Draper.
Arrangement Ralph Vaughan Williams © Oxford University Press, 70 Baker Street, London W1M 1DJ, UK.

Call to Holiness

Leader: I saw the Lord seated on a throne, high and exalted, and the skirt of his robe filled the temple. Seraphim were in attendance on him. Each had six wings: with one pair of wings they covered their faces and with another their bodies, and with the third pair they flew. They were calling to one another,

"Holy, holy, holy is the Lord of Hosts
the whole earth is full of his glory." (Isa. 6:1b-3)

Sanctus and Benedictus *(sung a cappella)*

The Iona Community: United Kingdom

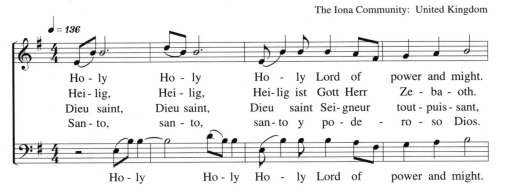

name of the Lord. Bless - ed, bless- ed
Na - men des Herrn. Preist ihn, preist ihn
nom du Sei - gneur. Bé - ni, bé - ni
nom - bre de Dios. Fe - liz, fe - liz

name of the Lord. Bless - ed Bless - ed,

is he who comes in the name of the Lord. Ho- san - na in the
der da kommt im Na - men des Herrn. Ho- san - na in der
ce - lui qui vient au nom du Sei - gneur. Ho- san - na dans les
es el que vie - ne en el nom - bre de Dios. Ho- sa- na en las al-

is he who comes in the name of the Lord

high - est. Ho - san- na in the high - est.
Hö - he. Ho - san- na in der Hö - he.
hauts cieux. Ho - san- na dans les hauts cieux.
tu- ras. Ho - sa- na en las al - tu- ras.

Ho - san- na in the high - est   Ho - san- na in the high- est

Offering of Incense (sit)

Leader: As each called, the threshold shook to its foundations at the sound, while the house began to fill with clouds of smoke. (Isa. 6:4)

(During the offering of the incense the following words from Psalm 141:2 will be sung, "Let my prayer rise before you as incense, the lifting up of my hands as an evening sacrifice")

Psalm 141:2

I-to Loh: Taiwan

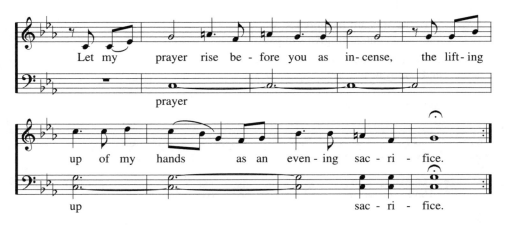

Let my prayer rise be - fore you as in - cense, the lift- ing

prayer

up of my hands as an even - ing sac - ri - fice.

up sac - ri - fice.

Call to Confession

Leader: Then I said, "Woe is me! I am doomed,
for my own eyes have seen the King, the Lord of Hosts,
I, a man of unclean lips,
I, who dwell among a people of unclean lips." (Isa. 6:5)

Prayer of Confession

Leader: If we have been singing praises with our voices,
and kept the joy out of our hearts —

If we have written reports concerning the marginalized,
and have kept them outside our gates —

Response *(sung a cappella)*

Urdu

R. F. Liberius: Pakistan

♩ = 88

1,3. Khu- da - ya, ra - hem kar. Khu- da - ya, ra hem, -
Have mer - cy on us, Lord, have mer - cy on us.

Khu- da - ya, ra - hem kar. Khu- da - ya, ra - hem.
Have mer - cy on us, Lord, have mer - cy on us.

fine

Khu— da - ya, ra - hem kar, khu- da - ya, ra - hem.
Have mer - cy on us, Lord, have mer - cy on us.

Leader: If we have met only with our ecumenical friends,
and totally ignored others —

If we have heard testimonies,
and been content to give sympathy —

If we have debated only to convince,
and not to hear —

Response: Khudaya

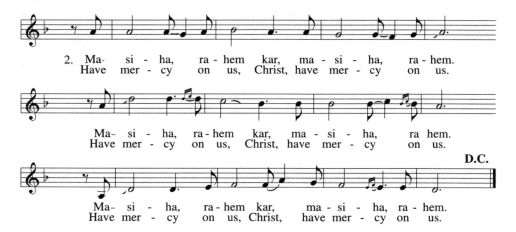

2. Ma- si - ha, ra - hem kar, ma - si - ha, ra - hem.
Have mer - cy on us, Christ, have mer - cy on us.

Ma- si - ha, ra - hem kar, ma - si - ha, ra hem.
Have mer - cy on us, Christ, have mer - cy on us.

D.C.

Ma- si - ha, ra - hem kar, ma - si - ha, ra - hem.
Have mer - cy on us, Christ, have mer - cy on us.

© I-to Loh, Tainan Theological Seminary, 117 Section 1, Tung Men Road, Tainan, Taiwan.

Leader: If we have prayed, "Giver of Life, Sustain your Creation",
and succumbed to the economics of consumption —
If we have prayed, "Spirit of Truth, Set us Free",
and chosen instead the slavery of silence —
If we have prayed, "Spirit of Unity, Reconcile your People",
and have not met with persons of other confessions or traditions in our own
neighbourhood
If we have prayed, "Holy Spirit, Transform and Sanctify us",
and not expected the Spirit to change our lives —

Response: Khudaya

Assurance of Forgiveness

Leader: One of the seraphim flew to me, carrying in his hand a glowing coal which he
had taken from the altar with a pair of tongs. He touched my mouth with it and
said,

"This has touched your lips;
now your iniquity is removed
and your sin is wiped out." (Isa. 6:6-7)

Leader: People of God, your guilt is taken away, and your sin forgiven.
People: Amen.

Entrance of the Word: Gloria, gloria, gloria (see p.121)

Epistle Reading: Galatians 5:13-14; 22-23

Alleluia *(sung a cappella)*

Russia

Al-le-lu - ja, Al-le-lu - ja,   Al-le-lu - ja!

Gospel Reading: John 3:5-8

Alleluia

Nicene-Constantinopolitan Creed

Call to Prayer

Leader: Sisters and brothers, is God's Spirit not present with us? Maybe we do not
experience God on a throne with thunder and lightning as Isaiah did; nevertheless [in the crackling of the wood] in this chapel, in the rising smoke of the
incense, in the sound of our singing, in our nearness to one another, does not the
Spirit of God move over us claiming us and calling us to new life?

Now, in silence, God leads us. The wind of the Spirit blows where it wills.
We remember that the Spirit blows not only through the church and the world,
but through our personal lives as well. The Spirit may convict or comfort,
strengthen or question. But will not leave us alone.

Within this circle of quiet, let us commit ourselves to pray for each other.
You are invited to turn to your neighbour and share with them one thing for
which you would like them to remember you in prayer. Your request may be
personal, or for your church, or your community.

Response: Come, Holy Spirit

Per Harling: Sweden

Intercessions

Leader: Come, Holy Spirit, renew the whole creation.
          Send the wind and flame of your transforming life
          to lift up the church in this day.
          Give wisdom and faith that we may know
          the great hope to which we are called.

          Response: Come, Holy Spirit

Leader: Giver of life,
          sustain your creation.
          Confront us with our greedy consuming of your gifts.
          Stand before us as we pillage and destroy.
          Call us forth into new harmonies of care
          for all that lives and breathes and has its being.

          Response: Come, Holy Spirit

Leader: Spirit of truth,
set us free to emerge as the children of God.
Open our ears that we may hear the weeping of the world.
Open our mouths that we may be a voice for the voiceless,
Open our eyes that we may see your vision
of peace and justice.
Make us alive with the courage and faith
of your prophetic truth.

Response: Come, Holy Spirit

Leader: Spirit of unity,
Reconcile your people.
Give us the wisdom to hold to what we need
to be your church.
Give us the grace to lay down
those things that you can do without.
Give us a vision of your breadth and length and height
which will challenge our smallness of heart
and bring us humbly together.

Response: Come, Holy Spirit

Leader: Holy Spirit,
transform and sanctify us
as we take up this task in your name.
Give us the gifts we need to be your church
in spirit and in truth.

Response: Come, Holy Spirit

Lord's Prayer (in your own language)

Passing the Peace (stand)

Blessing

Leader: May God Almighty bless you,
blessings of heaven above
blessings of the deep lying below
blessings of the breasts and womb
blessings of the grain and flowers
blessings of the eternal mountains
bounty of the everlasting hills. (Gen. 49:25-26)
Be with you and go with you until we meet again.
In the name of the Father, Son and Holy Spirit.
People: Amen.

Sending Forth

Leader: I heard the Lord saying, "Whom shall I send? Who will go for us?" (Isa. 6:8)
People: Here am I! Send me.

Hymn *(sung a cappella)*

South Africa

Lead me Lord (3x)
lead me Jesus.

Fill me.
Use me

Seng' ya vuma (3x)
Somandla.

I will go Lord, (3x)
In your name, Lord, I will go.

Führe mich Herr (3x)
führ' mich Herr.
Fülle mich.

Seng' ya vuma (3x)
Somandla.

Guide-moi Seigneur
Guide-moi Jésus (3x)
oui guide-moi.
Change-moi.

Seng' ya vuma (3x)
Somandla.

Guíame Dios
Lléname de tu poder.

Seng' ya vuma (3x)
Somandla.

Yo iré, Dios (3x)
En tu nombre yo iré.

Service of Remembrance:
"Holy Spirit — Transform and Sanctify Us"

This service would be appropriate for All Saints or memorial services. It was celebrated the first time in the chapel of the Ecumenical Centre in Geneva during a central committee meeting (another version of it was celebrated in Canberra 1991). The front of the chapel was prepared by hanging many large pictures of historical and contemporary people (both icons and photographs), well known and unknown, who, by faith and in their lives, have witnessed the power of the gospel and have reflected the image of God. In a local situation one might use pictures of persons from that place. The walls of the chapel were hung with large pieces of paper, covered with some small icons/photographs. The scripture reading this morning was from Hebrews 11, which tells the story of the people of faith in the biblical journey. At the end of the reading people were invited to remember the persons of faith whom they had met in their own faith journey and to write the names of those persons on the papers on the walls. When this had been done, the continuation from Hebrews was read, the beginning of chapter 12: "Therefore, since we are surrounded by so great a cloud of witnesses, let us also lay aside..."

One personal memory: Walking round and looking at the wall papers afterwards I experienced something significant — independent of time and culture — of how faith comes by faith. The most common name of all on the papers was: "My mother." The most important evangelist is the praying mother.....

If the service has become meaningful, that meaning should not be destroyed by insensitively taking the papers down immediately after the service.

* * *

Call to Worship (stand)

Leader: Sisters and brothers — arise
          Arise and lift your hearts
          Arise and lift your eyes
          Arise and lift your voices!

People: The living God,
          the living, moving Spirit of God
          has called us together —

in witness,
in celebration,
in struggle.

Leader: Reach out towards each other,
for our God reaches out towards us!
Let us worship God!

Sanctus and Benedictus (see pp.142-144) *(sung a cappella)*

New Testament Reading: Hebrews 11 — selected verses (sit)

Leader: Now faith is the assurance of things hoped for, the conviction of things not seen. By faith we understand that the world was created by the word of God, so that what is seen was made out of things which do not appear.

By faith Abel offered to God a more acceptable sacrifice than Cain. By faith Noah, being warned by God concerning events as yet unseen, took heed and constructed an ark for the saving of his household.

By faith Abraham obeyed when he was called to go out to a place which he was to receive as an inheritance, and he went out, not knowing where he was to go.

By faith Sarah herself received power to conceive, even when she was past the age, since she considered him faithful who had promised.

By faith Abraham, when he was tested, offered up Isaac, and he who had received the promises was ready to offer up his only son.

By faith Moses, when he was born, was hid for three months by his parents.

By faith Moses, when he was grown up, refused to be called the son of Pharaoh's daughter, choosing rather to share ill-treatment with the people of God.

By faith the people crossed the Red Sea as if on dry land.

By faith Rahab the harlot did not perish with those who were disobedient, because she had given friendly welcome to the spies.

And what more shall I say? For time would fail me to tell of Gideon, Barak, Samson, Jephthah, of David and Samuel and the prophets — who through faith conquered kingdoms, enforced justice, received promises, stopped the mouths of lions, quenched raging fire, escaped the edge of the sword, won strength out of weakness.

Reflection

Leader: Sisters and brothers, the scriptures remind us that our spiritual ancestors lived by faith. There is not time to give an account of all of them. By faith, many, known and unknown, have been the reflection of God's glory and righteousness; by faith many have gathered together to be the church; to be the image of God for their neighbours and the world.

These heavenly friends have kept the faith alive. They have mirrored what it means to be transformed and sanctified. They have witnessed to us the power of living the gospel.

Each of us has been touched by such a person of faith. Take a moment to remember:

Who has brought your faith alive?
Who has witnessed to you the Christian story?
Who has shone with God's grace so that you could believe?

Silence

Remembering these persons, you are now invited to write their names on the paper on the walls.

Song (during which people move to the papers on the walls): Thuma mina (see pp. 150-151) *(sung a cappella)*

Words of Assurance

Leader: Therefore, since we are surrounded by so great a cloud of witnesses, let us also lay aside every weight, and sin which clings so closely, and let us run with perseverance the race that is set before us, looking to Jesus the pioneer and perfecter of our faith, who for the joy that was set before him endured the cross, despising the shame, and is seated at the right hand of the throne of God. (Heb. 12:1,2)

Response: Gloria, gloria, gloria (see p. 121) (stand)

Intercessory Prayers

Leader: How great is your faithfulness, O God.
People: Call us forth in new faithfulness to you.

Leader: Lift us up on the wings of your Spirit,
through pathways that lead to your reign.
Move us beyond the edge of our dreams.
People: How great is your faithfulness, O God.
Call us forth in new faithfulness to you.

Leader: Sweep us forward like an ocean of truth,
breaking free of the power of self-interest
until the whole earth sings with your justice.
People: How great is your faithfulness, O God.
Call us forth in new faithfulness to you.

Leader: Burn us clean with the fire of your love
that we may rise up as the children of God,
walking bravely towards the cross of our day.
People: How great is your faithfulness, O God.
Call us forth in new faithfulness to you.

Leader: Breathe in us the breath of your Spirit,
that your risen life may be seen in our witness
as we join hands with the faithful of every age.
People: How great is your faithfulness, O God.
Call us forth in new faithfulness to you.

Lord's Prayer (in your own language)

Blessing

Leader: The Lord is the Spirit, and where the Spirit of the Lord is, there is freedom. And we all, with unveiled face, belonging to the glory of the Lord, are being changed into his likeness from one degree of glory to another; for this comes from the Lord, who is the Spirit.

Leader: May the Lord bless us and keep us.
May the Lord lift up the light of his
countenance upon us and give us peace,
this day and for ever more.

People: Amen, thanks be to God.

Closing Song: Thuma mina (see pp.150-151) *(sung a cappella)*

6. Lima Liturgy

The work on church unity has found many expressions in the ecumenical movement. One of the most notable is the Lima document, named after the Faith and Order commission meeting in Lima, Peru, in 1982, which finally came to an agreement on the document *Baptism, Eucharist and Ministry* (the BEM document) after twenty years of consultations, revisions and preparations. At the Lima conference a eucharist, specially composed on the basis of the BEM document, was celebrated. The main author of the Lima liturgy was brother Max Thurian from the ecumenical community of Taizé. "In composing the liturgy for the Lima conference, my aim was to illustrate the solid theological achievements of the Faith and Order document *Baptism, Eucharist and Ministry*... No 'authority' attaches to this particular liturgy, save that accruing to it from the fact of its having been used on certain significant ecumenical occasions" (*Baptism and Eucharist: Ecumenical Convergence in Celebration*, eds M. Thurian & G. Wainwright, Geneva, WCC, 1983, p.241.)

The Lima liturgy has been widely used — and translated into many languages — in different ecumenical circles, especially since it was celebrated at the WCC's sixth assembly in Vancouver in 1983. The structure — introduction, liturgy of the Word and liturgy of the eucharist — follows the universal Christian tradition known from the first Christian church. It is an important ecumenical, liturgical expression with its openness to Roman Catholic tradition and its attempt to overcome classical disagreements in Western and Eastern traditions, for instance in using the Nicene-Constantinopolitan Creed without the Western additions of "God from God" in the second article and "and the Son" *(filioque)* in the third article. At the same time a eucharist celebration of this kind underlines the painful realization that in the ecumenical movement we still cannot share the body and blood of Christ at the same table.

At the Canberra assembly an adapted form of the Lima liturgy was used. The structure is more or less the same (an Orthodox "Trisagion" is used for instance instead of "Gloria"), but the music and some wordings are new.

* * *

Opening Hymn

Martin Rinckart

Johann Crüger: Germany

der gro - ße Din - ge tut an uns und al - len En - den,
who won- drous things has done, in whom this world re - joic - es;
Et joi- gnons no - tre voix au con - cert des saints an - ges!

der uns von Mut - ter - leib und Kin - des- bei- nen an un -
who from our moth- ers' arms has blessed us on our way with
Dès les bras ma - ter - nels il nous a pro - té - gés et

zäh - lig viel zu - gut und noch jetzt und ge - tan..
count- less gifts of love, and still is ours to - day.
jus - qu'au der - nier jour, il est no - tre ber - ger.

2. Der ewigreiche Gott
woll uns bei unserm Leben
ein immer fröhlich Herz
und edlen Frieden geben
und uns in seiner Gnad
erhalten fort und fort
und uns aus aller Not
erlösen hier und dort.

2. O may this bounteous God
through all our life be near us,
with ever joyful hearts
and blessed peace to cheer us;
and keep us still in grace,
and guide us when perplexed;
and free us from all ills,
in this world and the next.

2. Loué soit notre Dieu!
Que notre vie entière
tous nous vivions joyeux
sous le regard du Père,
qu'il nous tienne en sa grâce,
et nous guide toujours,
nous garde du malheur
par son unique amour.

3. Lob, Ehr und Preis sei Gott,
dem Vater und dem Sohne
und dem, der beiden gleich
im höchsten Himmelsthrone,
dem dreimal einen Gott,
wie es ursprünglich war
und ist und bleiben wird
jetzt und und immerdar.

3. All praise and thanks
   to God
the Father now be given;
the Son, and him who reigns
with them in highest heaven;
the one eternal God,
whom earth and heaven adore;
for thus it was, is now,
and shall be evermore.

3. De ce Dieu trois fois saint
qui règne dans la gloire,
chrétiens empressons-nous
de chanter la victoire;
son Royaume est aux cieux
où plein de majesté,
il règne, seul vrai Dieu,
de toute éternité.

English, Catherine Winkworth. French, F. du Pasquier.

Greeting

Leader: The grace of our Lord Jesus Christ,
         the love of God,
         and the communion of the Holy Spirit
         be with you all.
People: And also with you.

Confession

People: Most merciful God,
         we confess that we are in bondage to sin
         and cannot free ourselves.
         We have sinned against you in thought, word and deed
         by what we have done and by what we have left undone.
         We have not loved you with our whole heart;
         we have not loved our neighbours as ourselves.
         For the sake of your Son, Jesus Christ,
         have mercy on us.
         Forgive us, renew us and lead us
         so that we may delight in your will
         and walk in your ways,
         to the glory of your holy name. Amen.

Leader: Almighty God
         gave Jesus Christ to die for us
         and for the sake of Christ forgives us all our sins.
         I therefore declare to you
         the forgiveness of your sins,
         in the name of the Father, and of the Son,
         and of the Holy Spirit.
People: Amen.

Trisagion (see p.42) *(sung a cappella)*

Opening Prayer

Leader: Almighty God,
         who on the day of Pentecost
         sent your Holy Spirit to the disciples
         with the wind from heaven and in tongues of flame,
         filling them with joy and boldness to preach the gospel;
         send us out in the power of the same Spirit
         to witness to your truth
         and to draw all people to the fire of your love,
         through Jesus Christ our Lord
         who lives and reigns with you,
         in the unity of the Holy Spirit,
         ever one God, world without end.
People: Amen.

Liturgy of the Word (sit)

First Reading: Acts 2:1-11

Psalter: Psalm 104:26-32

Psalm Response (at the beginning, after v.30 and at the end)

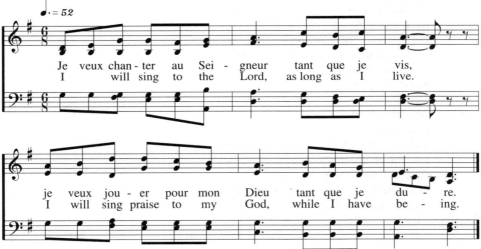

D. Rimaud harmonized by J. Berthier: France

Je veux chan-ter au Sei - gneur tant que je vis,
I will sing to the Lord, as long as I live.

je veux jou - er pour mon Dieu tant que je du - re.
I will sing praise to my God, while I have be - ing.

Gospel Procession (stand)

Hallelujah (see pp.76-77)

Gospel Reading: John 20:19-23

Homily (sit)

Silence

Nicene-Constantinopolitan Creed (stand)

Leader: Let us affirm our faith together.
People: We believe in one God, the Father, the Almighty,
        maker of heaven and earth, of all that is, seen and unseen.

We believe in one Lord, Jesus Christ, the only Son of God,
eternally begotten of the Father, Light from Light,
true God from true God, begotten, not made,
of one Being with the Father;
through him all things were made.
For us and for our salvation he came down from heaven;
by the power of the Holy Spirit he became incarnate
from the Virgin Mary and was made man.
For our sake he was crucified under Pontius Pilate;
he suffered death and was buried;
on the third day he rose again in accordance with the scriptures;
he ascended into heaven.
He is seated at the right hand of the Father,
he will come again in glory
to judge the living and the dead,
and his kingdom will have no end.

We believe in the Holy Spirit, the Lord, the giver of life,
who proceeds from the Father;
with the Father and the Son he is worshipped and glorified;
he has spoken through the prophets.
We believe in one holy catholic and apostolic church.
We acknowledge one baptism for the forgiveness of sins.
We look for the resurrection of the dead,
and the life of the world to come. Amen.

Intercessions (seated)

Leader: In the power of the Spirit and in union with
Christ, let us pray:

Response *(sung a cappella)*

Korean   Jacques Berthier: Taizé, France

Chu-yo   chu - yo   tu-ro   chu-so-so.   Chu-yo   chu— yo   tu-ro   chu-so-so.

Lord hear us. Höre uns, Gott. Seigneur, écoute-nous. Señor, escúchanos.

Music J. Berthier © Ateliers et Presses de Taizé, 71250 Taizé, France.

Leader: Govern and direct your holy church;
fill it with love and truth;
and grant us that unity which is your will.

Response: Hear us

Leader: Give us the boldness to preach the gospel in all the world;
         enlightening our knowledge and understanding
         that our teaching and our lives may proclaim your word.

         Response: Hear us

Leader: Guide the leaders of the nations
         in the ways of peace and justice.

         Response: Hear us

Leader: Keep in safety those who travel and those in danger
         and care for the sick, the homeless, the hungry, the prisoners,
         and all who are in trouble and oppressed.

         Response: Hear us

Leader: Hear us as we remember those who have died
         in the peace of Christ,
         both those who have confessed the faith
         and those whose faith is known to you alone,
         and grant us with them a share in your eternal kingdom.

         Response: Hear us

Leader: Holy God, you hear those who pray in the name of your Son
         grant that what we have asked in faith
         we may obtain according to your will;
         through Jesus Christ our Lord.
People: Amen.

Liturgy of the Eucharist

Offertory

Song

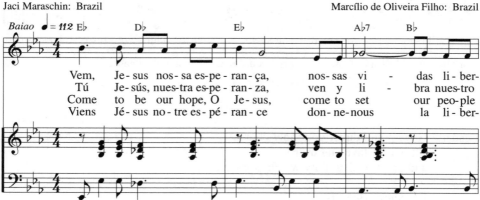

Jaci Maraschin: Brazil

Marcílio de Oliveira Filho: Brazil

2. Vem tecer um mundo novo
nos caminhos da verdade;
para que, afinal, o povo
viva em plena liberdade.
Vem, Jesus, abre o futuro
do teu reino de alegria.
Vem, derruba o imenso muro
que separa a noite e o dia.

2. Come to build your new creation
through the road of servanthood;
give new life to every nation,
changing evil into good.
Come and open our tomorrow
for your joyful reign so near.
Take away all human sorrow,
give us hope against our fear.

2. Ven, y teje un mundo nuevo
caminando en la verdad,
para que, por fin, el pueblo
viva en plena libertad.
Ven, Jesús, abre el futuro
de tu Reino de alegría.
Ven, derrumba este gran muro
que hoy separa noche y día.

2. Viens ton monde renouvelle
fais régner la vérité
pour qu'enfin ton peuple vive
dans la sainte liberté.
Viens Jésus et que ton règne
nous apporte paix et joie.
Viens et détruis la muraille
qui nous sépare de toi.

Leader: Blessed are you, Lord God of the universe,
you are the giver of this bread,
fruit of the earth and of human labour,
let it become the bread of Life.

People: Blessed be God, now and for ever.

Leader: Blessed are you, Lord God of the universe,
you are the giver of this wine,
fruit of the vine and of human labour,
let it become the wine of the eternal kingdom.

People: Blessed be God, now and for ever.

Leader: As the grain once scattered in the fields
and the grapes once dispersed on the hillside
and now reunited on this table in bread and wine,
so, Lord, may your whole church soon be gathered together
from the corners of the earth into your kingdom.

Eucharistic Prayer

Leader: The Lord be with you
People: And also with you.

Leader: Lift up your hearts.
People: We lift them to the Lord.

Leader: Let us give thanks to the Lord our God.
People: It is right to give God thanks and praise.

Leader: Truly it is right and good to glorify you,
at all times and in all places,
to offer you our thanksgiving, O Lord, Holy Father,
Almighty and Everlasting God.
Through your living Word you created all things,
and pronounced them good.
You made human beings in your own image,
to share your life and reflect your glory.
When the time had fully come,
you gave Christ to us as the Way, the Truth and the Life.
He accepted baptism and consecration as your Servant
to announce the good news to the poor.

We give you thanks because by the Holy Spirit
you lead us into all truth, and give us power
to proclaim your gospel to the nations,
and to serve you as a royal priesthood.

So, with the angels and all the saints,
we proclaim and sing your glory:

Sanctus (see pp.65-67)

Leader: O God, Lord of the universe,
you are holy and your glory is beyond measure.
We are grateful that
Christ bequeathed to us the eucharist,
that we should celebrate the memorial
of the cross and resurrection,
and receive his presence as food.
May this Creator Spirit accomplish the words
of your beloved Son,
who, on the night in which he was betrayed,
took bread, and when he had given thanks to you,
broke it and gave it to his disciples, saying:
Take, eat: this is my body,
which is given for you.
Do this for the remembrance of me.
After supper he took the cup
and when he had given thanks,
he gave it to them and said:
Drink this, all of you:
this is my blood of the new covenant,
which is shed for you and for many
for the forgiveness of sins.
Do this for the remembrance of me.

Response *(sung quietly during the following prayers)*

Jacques Berthier: Taizé, France

♩· = 56

Ve - ni San - cte Spi - ri - tus.

Come Holy Spirit. Komm, Heiliger Geist. Viens, Saint Esprit. Ven, Espíritu Santo

Leader: Gracious God,
        we celebrate today the memorial of our redemption:
        we recall the birth and life of your Son among us,
        his death and descent to the abode of the dead.
        We proclaim Christ's resurrection and ascension in glory,
        where as our Great High Priest
        he ever intercedes for all people;
        and we look for his coming at the last.

        Behold, Lord, this eucharist
        which you yourself gave to the church,
        and graciously receive it,
        as you accept the offering of your Son
        whereby we are reinstated in your covenant.

        Upon this eucharist send your life-giving Spirit.
        May the outpouring of this Spirit of Fire
        transfigure this thanksgiving meal
        that this bread and wine may become for us
        the body and blood of Christ.

        As we partake of Christ's body and blood,
        fill us with the Holy Spirit
        that we may be one body and one spirit in Christ,
        a living sacrifice to the praise of your glory.

        Remember Loving God,
        your one, holy, catholic and apostolic church,
        redeemed by the blood of Christ.
        Reveal its unity, guard its faith,
        and preserve it in peace.
        Remember, all the servants of your church
        bishops, presbyters, deacons,
        and all to whom you have given special gifts of ministry.

Remember also all our sisters and brothers
who have died in the peace of Christ,
and those whose faith is known to you alone
guide them to the joyful feast prepared
for all peoples in your presence,
with the blessed Virgin Mary,
with the patriarchs and prophets, the apostles and martyrs.
and all the saints for whom your friendship was life.
With all these we sing your praise
and await the happiness of your kingdom
where with the whole creation,
finally delivered from sin and death,
we shall be enabled to glorify you
through Christ our Lord.

Through Christ, with Christ, in Christ,
all honour and glory is yours.
Almighty God and Father,
in the unity of the Holy Spirit,
now and for ever.

Amen

Chinese folk melody, arr. Puqi Jiang: China

A-men   A - men   A - men.   A-men   A- men   A - men.

Music © Puqi Jiang, The Asian School of Music, Worship and the Arts, P.O. Box 10533 Broadway Centrum, Quezon City 1112 Philippines.

Lord's Prayer (in your own language) (stand)

Leader: United by one baptism
in the same Holy Spirit and the same body of Christ,
we pray as God's sons and daughters:

People: Our Father...

The Peace

Leader: Lord Jesus Christ, you told your apostles:
Peace I leave with you, my peace I give to you.
Look not on our sins but on the faith of your church;
In order that your will be done,
grant us always this peace and guide us
towards the perfect unity of your kingdom for ever.

People: Amen.

Leader: The peace of the Lord be with you always.

People: And also with you.

Leader: Let us give one another a sign of reconciliation and peace.

Song *(sung a cappella during the exchange of the peace)*

From "Missa da Terra Sem Males"   D. Pedro Casaldáliga, Pedro Tierra,
                                       Martin Coplas: Guarany, Brazil-Paraguay

Peace Friede Paix Paz Pace

Breaking of the Bread

Leader: The bread which we break
is the communion of the body of Christ;
the cup of blessing for which we give thanks
is the communion in the blood of Christ.

Lamb of God

Matti Rantatalo: Finland

Musical notation with lyrics:

tä.
cy.

Oi   Ju-ma-lan Ka - rit - sa, io-ka
O,   Lamb   God,   you that

pois o-tat maa il-man syn - - - nin,   an - na'
take a - way the world's   sin: grant   us

meil-le   rau-ha - si   ja siu-na - uk - se - si.
peace,   grant us jus-tice,   grant us your own true peace.

Communion *(during which congregational songs are sung)*

Thanksgiving Prayer

Leader: In peace let us pray to the Lord.
O Lord our God, we give you thanks
for uniting us by baptism in the body of Christ
and for filling us with joy in the eucharist.
Lead us towards the full visible unity of your church
and help us to treasure all the signs of reconciliation you have granted us.
Now that we have tasted of the banquet
you have prepared for us in the world to come,
may we all one day share together the inheritance of the saints
in the life of your heavenly city,
through Jesus Christ, your Son, our Lord,
who lives and reigns with you in the unity of the Holy Spirit,
ever one God, world without end.

People: Amen.

Blessing

Leader: The Spirit of truth lead you into all truth,
         give you grace to confess that Jesus Christ is Lord,
         and to proclaim the word and works of God;
         and the blessing of God Almighty, Father, Son and Holy Spirit,
         be with you now and forever.
People: Amen.

Word of Mission

Leader: You shall receive power
         when the Holy Spirit has come upon you;
         and you shall be my witnesses.
People: Thanks be to God.

Closing Song: Masithi (see p.75) *(sung a cappella)*

7. Walking the Way of the Cross

This meditation walk, done early on the third morning of the world mission conference in San Antonio in 1989, endeavoured to bring the two parts of the conference theme — "Your will be done — Mission in Christ's way" — together in an individually experienced way, by inviting people to walk the way of Christ in solidarity with the suffering people of today. Over a period of three hours, a continuous flow of some 800 people (starting at different times during the early morning), each at his/her own pace, moved quietly and solemnly through the walk. The following guide, which each person received as a meditational "map" of the walk, with reflections from people in many parts of the world, enabled participants to focus on the themes of each place of meditation. To many this walk was the most powerful experience of the conference.

The walk went through nine stations in the university campus area. At each station (and between them to show the way) assistants helped people in the different symbolic actions. Making the walk work required considerable preparation, which is natural as so many people took part in it. Since San Antonio, though, the walk has been used in many smaller situations and with less people involved and it has worked quite well. It is not necessary to use all the stations. The first (use the bowls of ashes at the second station) and the last station can easily be taken away. The walk could be used as preparation for a service (e.g. on Good Friday), which might end in the chapel with a short liturgy; the large beam of wood from station 5 — with the sheets of paper nailed to it — may be taken in procession to the front, the paper taken off and burned. People may be invited to come to the baptismal font, where the crosses in their foreheads may be washed off as a kind of absolution. If this happens on Good Friday station 8 should not be used.

Items needed

Signs to show the way.

Station 1: (1) 4 murals or pictures with scenes from the life of Christ, illustrating how his life was lived in solidarity with the poor and oppressed; (2) bowls of ashes.

Station 2: (1) Placard(s) with the words of Jesus, "Not my will, but yours be done", perhaps in several languages.

Station 3: (1) Large photographs of suffering people and of people in forsaken situations. These can be asked for from local newspapers and/or mission boards; (2) two-three big wooden crosses; (3) tape recorder, and a pre-recorded tape with sounds which may be obtained from a local radio station; there are also sound banks available on CDs and tapes.

Station 4: (1) Large pieces of paper with names (and maybe photographs) of people who have been condemned to die because of their faith. These may be available from mission boards, Amnesty International, etc.; (2) pitchers of water and towels.

Station 5: (1) Large beam of wood; (2) nails and hammers; (3) pieces of paper and pens.

Station 6: (1) Wine and vinegar; (2) small paper cups; (3) scarves for blindfolding.

Station 7: (1) A large wooden cross; (2) votive candles and flowers.

Station 8: (1) Water and napkins; (2) icon of the resurrection or resurrection pictures (votive candles and flowers).

Station 9: Simple bread and water.

The following guide was given to people as they arrived at the starting point. (Text in bold type is added here to explain the surroundings and the liturgical action at each station.)

Walking the Way of the Cross — a Meditation Guideline

People were invited to come to a parking area, where they received this guide and a map of the walk. They simply had to follow the signs, which showed the way through the different stations.

Foreword

Welcome to this early morning; we pray that this will be a meaningful, if somewhat unusual experience in which we are open to personal and communal reflection on suffering in our world and its relationship to our commitment to "mission in Christ's way". The walk is not an end in itself; our getting up early is not per se a meaningful act of solidarity. But we trust that our experience may lead to acts of obedience to God's will that express, in our lives and in our mission, the solidarity with the poor and oppressed that characterized Jesus' ministry.

The walk is arranged for maximum freedom of participation; you are invited to follow the map, pausing before or at the numbered places on the map to read the text which corresponds to that number. You may set your own pace; perhaps you will occasionally want to find a spot to sit and to reflect and pray. You may walk alone, or in the company of a few persons with whom you wish to share your thoughts.

You are also invited in each place to a specific action; you are free to respond or not. The physical movement, the visual images, the sounds, the possibilities to taste and to feel are all invitations to enter with all our senses — not only with our minds — into a fuller understanding of what it means in today's world to walk the way of the cross.

Please read the introduction before moving to the starting point, where helpers will indicate when you may begin the walk.

Introduction

When people discover that I have been imprisoned four times in the last ten years in South Korea, they think it very strange and ask me: "What crimes has a minister committed, that he has gone to jail several times?"

But I do not think it at all strange that a minister, or a Christian, should go to jail frequently. This is the more so as I read the Bible and study the last two thousand years' history of the Christian church. Jesus' leading disciple, Peter, was dragged off to jail twice and Paul three times — and Paul remained imprisoned for a long time. Jesus himself was arrested by the Roman soldiers, tried and executed.

The cross of which we Christians boast, which we hang around our necks and with which we decorate our churches — is it not the symbol of horrible execution? Where is the path that the Lord trod? If we are disciples, he does not allow us any other path than the path of following him bearing the cross. So I cannot abandon this path — I have tried to walk along it.

Whenever I felt pain and difficulty in the jail or in the workers' struggle, I remembered the way of the cross of Christ. In that hard suffering — at times even suffering the pain of facing death — I experienced a sense of participating in the suffering of Christ, and felt a boundless joy. As we participate in the glory of Christ's resurrection.

We are limbs of Christ's body. Today in Latin America, in Africa, in Asia and in many other places throughout the world, our brothers and sisters are suffering. And Christ is suffering with them. If we cannot feel the suffering of these brothers and sisters, we are not the limbs of Christ's body. Or, if we are attached to the body, we (also) are diseased or have an impediment. We must feel the suffering which our brothers and sisters experience in many places in the world. Then we will also experience the joy of Christ's resurrection beyond the suffering.

There is no resurrection apart from the cross.
In Myung-Jin, South Korea

1. Meditation on the Life of Christ

Participants paused first in front of large murals which pictured scenes from the life of Christ, illustrating how he lived in solidarity with the poor and the oppressed. On leaving this station people were invited to put a cross on their foreheads from a bowl of ashes.

The murals focus our attention on the life of Christ — how it was lived in solidarity with the poor and how the actions of Christ led directly to the giving of his life on the cross. Taking up the cross is a daily challenge to the ways in which we live our lives, as well as to the great moments of choice. You are invited to reflect on how life identifies with the persons with whom Christ identified.

If the Lord's disciples keep silence when some of God's people are devalued because of their colour or sex or beliefs; when men and women are put in prison and tortured; when injustice and oppression stalk the world in pursuit of the innocent and powerless: the stones will shout aloud in El Salvador and in Southern Africa; they will shout aloud in Afghanistan and on the West Bank; they will shout aloud in South Korea and in Belfast; they will shout:

"He has lifted up the lowly, he has filled the hungry with good things, and sent the rich away with empty hands... Blessed are those who hunger and thirst to see right prevail. They shall be satisfied."

If the Lord's disciples keep silence when children die from hunger, and many more live crippled and stunted lives; when men and women feel the pain of their uselessness in the eyes of the world; when the necessities of life come as a grudging handout, and not as the generous sharing of God's good gifts: the stones will shout aloud in Calcutta and the Horn of Africa; in Brazil, in Britain and in the United States; they will shout in hospitals and schools and unemployment offices and silent factories; they will shout:

"I was hungry and you gave me food, a stranger and you welcomed me, sick and you cared for me, in prison and you visited me. When you did it for one of the least of my children, you did it for me. Blessed are the merciful. God will show mercy to them."

If the Lord's disciples keep quiet... the very stones will shout aloud: "Take up your cross and follow me."

Kathy Galloway

As you leave the area, you are invited to commit yourself to living the way of the cross by marking your forehead (or in mutual action with others) with the sign of the cross in ashes.

2. Meditation in Gethsemane

Walking by a beautiful garden where a person knelt in prayer the participants could read the words of Jesus — "Not my will, but yours be done" — written in many languages on big placards.

The words of Jesus — "Not my will, but yours be done" — surround the area. You are invited to contemplate the struggle of Jesus in Gethsemane to pray this prayer to his father.

> "Not my will, Father, but yours be done." In the garden, Jesus was faced with a choice. He knew he had angered the religious rulers and he knew that he would not be able to count on his followers or the crowd for much support. He could try to escape from Jerusalem and avoid the coming confrontation. He could face the trial and try to reach a compromise with Caiaphas or Pilate. He could try to rally the common people to take up arms to protect him. But none of these choices would have fulfilled the Father's desire to reveal his unswerving love and his uncompromising opposition to inhuman violence and oppression. In accepting his Father's will, Jesus had at the same time to accept that he would be killed for what he was doing and saying. Indeed, he would be killed because of who he was.
>
> This was God's will. Not that he desired to see Jesus suffering and dying; not that he wanted the human race to be stained with the blood of the only truly innocent man ever born; but that he desired to show us the lengths to which he is prepared to go in forgiving us, in bearing our rejection, in sharing our sufferings. In this sense, then, we say that it was necessary for the Christ to suffer... There is nothing good about suffering; but there is something good in being prepared to accept it if it comes to us as part of our mission.
>
> Let us be very careful of our language, then, when we speak of the death of Jesus and God's will. Let us not disguise the fact that the death of Jesus was the killing of Jesus by ordinary people like ourselves... Let us not forget that the innocent are still condemned as he was; that those who speak against corruption, injustice and hypocrisy are still sent to their death every day. God does not want this to happen any more than God wanted Pilate to condemn Jesus to a shameful execution. However, God did want Jesus to be ready to bear with forgiveness even the unjust death which would be inflicted upon him by those who thought themselves close to God. Only in this way could we come to know of his extraordinary love.
>
> *Dan Madijan, SJ*

After Gethsemane, can we pray for God's will to be done on earth without reflection on and commitment to the personal and communal cost of that prayer? You are invited to make this prayer your own.

3. Meditation on Scourging and Mocking

As they approached this station participants could hear the sounds of war and violence from a prepared tape that was continuously played all through the walk. After walking by photographs of people in different suffering situations, participants were invited to carry, together with others, a large wooden cross. Assistants continuously carried back the three crosses that were used.

As you contemplate pictures of the suffering and oppression of the people of the world, you confront the powers which mock God's reign, which continue to "perfect" the cross of suffering imposed on people.

Your cross, O Lord
was too simple.
We had to perfect it:
large-caliber machine guns,
nuclear warheads,
grenades and napalm
are so much more effective!

In that corner of the world
where you came and first said,
"Our Father",
we have refined your cross.
In that corner of the world
where Moses received the command
"Thou shalt not kill",
we are pulling the pins
on hand grenades
and mounting howitzers.
In that corner of the world
where Herod
displaced you and your mother,
we continue mass-producing
displaced persons.

And all over the world,
your cross is being improved:
in Vietnam,
it is a shell hole;
in Latin America,
in India or the Horn of Africa,
the bare ribs of little children.

In our homes,
your cross hangs on the wall, carefully polished
and inlaid with mother-of-pearl
a cross without a history,
terribly silent,
with a silence of judgment itself.
When we ask,
"Where did we see you
naked,
hungry
or imprisoned,
Lord?"
it will reply with silence:
a silence like that
of all the well-oiled, well-greased,
effective, quiet weapons
which crucify on God's earth
those who are poor and innocent,
like you
those who die
because a world full of Cains
refuses to be its brother's keeper,
those who die
because the ivory of plaster crucifixes
remain up on the wall,
while the sign of the cross
is being engraved in human flesh
right in our midst.
And we see nothing!

Adapted from "You call us together" by Pierre Griolet

You are invited to carry the cross, alone or with others. Feel the weight and the burden. In what ways does Jesus continue to carry the cross today?

4. Meditation in the Judgment Hall

"The way of the cross" went through a large hall. The walls were covered with hundreds of names (and some photographs) of historical and present-day "martyrs". As people went through the hall the names were read in an ongoing litany. Participants were also invited to write new and maybe "unknown" names on the wall. By the end of the walk the papers were full of names... Outside the hall there was a table with a bowl of water and a towel; one participants wrote after the walk: "Privileged and protected, yet unable to wash my hands of responsibility. The towels around the bucket of water were shouting at me. I wanted to touch them — to see if they were damp from use or just arranged to look if they had been used. Am I called to join Pilate in the washing of hands? No! Mission in Christ's way means taking responsibility."

The walls of this judgment hall are inscribed with the names of those who have been condemned to die for their kingdom actions. Listen to the litany of the condemned...

Even today Jesus is condemned to death: when people cry for freedom, and they are accused of being terrorists; when people speak out the truth, and they are accused of being traitors; when people do good, and they are accused of being self-seekers...

And also when people fail to lift up their voices in support of truth.

I am no longer afraid of death,
I know well
its dark and cold corridors
leading to life.

I am afraid rather of that life
which does not come out of death,
which cramps our hands
and retards our march.

I am afraid of my fear
and even more of the fear of others,
who do not know where they are going,
who continue clinging
to what they consider to be life,
which we know to be death!

I live each day to kill death;
I die each day to beget life,
and in this dying unto death,
I die a thousand times
and am reborn another thousand
through that love from my People,
which nourishes hope!

Julia Esquivel, written in exile from Guatemala

You are invited to write on the papers on the wall the names of persons whom you have known who have suffered for righteousness' sake.

As you leave the hall, you will pass a bowl of water and a towel. "When Pilate saw that he was gaining nothing, but rather that a riot was beginning, he took water and washed his hands before the crowd, saying, 'I am innocent of this man's blood; see to it yourselves.'" Pause to reflect on our responsibility as Christians in the judgment halls of our world.

Can we wash our hands of this responsibility?

5. *Meditation on Nailing*

The sound of hammering echoed across the university campus in the early morning hours. As participants approached this station, where a large beam of wood was laid out, they were handed a nail and invited to write their personal or communal sins on a piece of paper and nail it to the wood. A large quantity of pens, paper and hammers were available.

The sound of nails being hammered into wood... these sounds remind us of those who are being crucified today by unjust economic policies, by military and political oppression, by discrimination, by unfettered greed, by the denial of basic human needs. Reflect on these as you hold a nail in your hands.

> I drive nails when I ignore the suffering that takes place far away from me in India, Latin America, Africa, Bosnia, Ireland, ... and nearby in ......
> I drive nails when my life-style means the oppression of my brothers and sisters in other parts of the world.
> I drive nails when I destroy a neighbour by revealing those secrets I know, those weaknesses I suspect.
> I drive nails when I think of myself as the one to be served..... and not the servant.

You are invited to identify other ways in which we, or our societies, crucify today.

Our Christian tradition includes the understanding that Jesus "was pierced for our transgressions, he was crushed for our iniquities; the punishment that brought us peace was upon him". You may wish to write down personal or communal sins and to nail the paper to the cross (or to hand it to those who are hammering), in this way acknowledging that "by his wounds we are healed".

6. *Meditation on Forsakenness*

On the way to the university chapel there were large photographs showing people in "forsaken" areas and situations. Among them there was a placard with the words of Jesus, "My God, my God, why have you forsaken me?" Outside the chapel people were invited to taste the bitterness of forsakenness by sipping some wine mixed with vinegar. Participants who were willing were blindfolded and led by assistants into the chapel, where they could sit down for a while, listening to the meditative music. After a while the blindfolds were taken off.

You are invited to reflect on the cry of Jesus, "My God, my God, why have you forsaken me?" In the world today there are many "forsaken" areas; the photographs show some of these, but many experiences of forsakenness can never be captured by a camera.

> Why, O why, Lord?
> You know our suffering;
> we are miserable and afflicted
> like the children of Israel in Egypt.
> And you are aware of it all.

Why, O why, Lord?
Why do you seem deaf to our doleful cries?
Or have you turned your back upon us?
Is our trust nothing to you, is our hope vain?
Why, why, why do you keep us waiting?

Why, O why, Lord?
Why did you tell us
that we were made in your image?
It might have been better
if you had let us alone in our blindness;
it would have been easier than to submit to our fate.
Why, Lord, did you open our eyes?

Why don't you answer when we cry out to you?
How long will you remain passive?
Why do you allow iniquity and lies to rule over us,
you who redeemed us at the cost of your own life?
You are King of kings
and yet they struck you with their fists;
they spat upon you to show their utter contempt!
Cruel nails pierced your hands and feet.
All this because of your great and infinite love for us.
Why, O why then are you silent?

From the depths we call to you:
save us in our distress!

Based on a contemporary psalm by Zephania Kameeta, Namibia

You are invited to taste the wine mixed with vinegar as the taste of the bitterness of forsakenness.

You are invited to walk the last part blindfolded to experience more fully the sense of helplessness and aloneness. Those who are willing to be blindfolded may put them on at this point; others may simply want to close their eyes. Let others around you assist you by grasping your hand and leading you into the chapel.

7. Meditation by the Cross

At the front of the chapel a large wooden cross was laid on the floor. Surrounding it were many votive candles. Meditative (Taizé) music was sung continuously. People were invited to kneel by the cross, lighting their own candles if they wished.

You are invited to kneel at the cross, surrounded by candles, and to meditate, or to sit as long as you wish in the chapel, reflecting on the meaning of the cross for mission in Christ's way in your life, your society and our world.

He was spurned and avoided by others,
a man of suffering, accustomed to infirmity,
one of those from whom people hide their faces.

Yet it was our infirmities that he bore,
our sufferings that he endured.
He was pierced for our offences,
crushed for our sins;
upon him was the chastisement that makes us whole,
by his stripes we were healed.
We had all gone astray like sheep,
each following his own way;
but the Lord laid upon him the guilt of us all.
Though he was harshly treated, he submitted;
he was silent and opened not his mouth.
Oppressed and condemned, he was taken away,
and who would have thought any more of his destiny?
When he was cut off from the land of the living,
and smitten for the sin of his people,
a place was assigned him among the wicked
and a burial place with evildoers,
though he had done no wrong
nor spoken any falsehood.
If he gives his life as an offering for sin,
he shall see his descendants in a long life,
and the will of the Lord shall be accomplished through him.
Because of his affliction
he shall see the light in fullness of days;
through his suffering, my servant shall justify many,
and their guilt he shall bear.
Therefore I give him his portion among the great,
and he shall divide the spoils with the mighty,
because he surrendered himself to death
and was counted among the wicked;
and he shall take the sins of many,
and win pardon for their offences.

Isaiah 53:3-12, abridged

8. Meditation on Resurrection

From the chapel the walk went into a small garden, where participants were invited to wash their foreheads at a fountain. In the garden was an Orthodox icon of the resurrection as well as contemporary depictions of the resurrection from various parts of the world. The sound of the water and the stillness and beauty of the garden made this place a powerful meditative sign of the new life in the resurrected Christ.

By entering the garden you are invited to cleanse your face in the fountain, remembering your baptism into the body of Christ. In the garden you can pause in front of the icon of the resurrection surrounded by flowers and other contemporary depictions of the resurrection from various parts of the world. You are invited to meditate on the hope of the resurrection for mission in Christ's way.

O death, where is your sting?
O Hades, where is your victory?
Christ is risen and you are abolished,
Christ is risen and the demons are cast down,
Christ is risen and the angels rejoice,
Christ is risen and life is freed,
Christ is risen and the tomb is emptied of the dead:
for Christ, being risen from the dead,
has become the Leader and Reviver
of those who had fallen asleep.
To Him be glory and power for ever and ever.

From John Chrysostom, fifth century

How strongly many Chinese Christians feared at the time of the liberation in 1949 that we were losing so many things dear to us... By all human reckoning Christianity, perhaps for the fourth time in Chinese history, was again breathing its last breath. What we were blind to was that when we were weak and young, life was in the offing. Strength is found in weakness, as life is dying...

Thus, we seem to understand Paul when he said, "We are afflicted in every way, but not crushed; perplexed, but not driven to despair; persecuted, but not forsaken; struck down, but not destroyed; always carrying in the body the death of Jesus, so that the life of Jesus may also be manifested in our bodies", and all this by the grace of God. A grain of wheat remains a grain if it does not get into the soil and die there; but if it does, it will bear many seeds.

We Christians have tried so often to wrap up the remains of Jesus Christ with the cloth we have brought. Others have tried so often to seal Jesus Christ up in his tomb with big, heavy stones, but the living Christ himself cannot be bound or enclosed. He broke out of any human-made tomb.

The resurrection truth tells us that it is through loss, poverty, suffering and death that life is attained, in nation as well as in church. It tells us life does not depend on power, wealth or property but on the risen Christ, the Lord of Life, who is also the ascended Christ, sitting at the right hand of God upholding the universe by his word of power.

K.H. Ting, China

9. Reflection on Shared Bread

So far no breakfast had been served. The last part of the walk went to the dining hall of the university. There people were offered a very simple breakfast of water and tortillas as an act of solidarity.

As you walk to the breakfast area, you may wish to recall the story of the disciples on the road to Emmaus: the disciples' intense discussion of current events with the stranger, Jesus opening the scriptures, showing that God brings life out of death, the recognition of Christ in the breaking of bread, and the eagerness of the disciples to run and tell others that they have encountered the risen Christ.

Shared bread is the experience of people as community,
and therefore the experience of God;
it is communion at once human and divine.
It is so all over the world;
it has been so all through the ages.
A central concern of Jesus is to promote table fellowship
and get people to share bread and life.

Shared food is concerted action to build community.
Community has its necessary material basis
in community of wealth,
in the common possession of the one earth.
Because the loaf of bread is one,
we, many though we are, are one body,
for we all partake of the one body.
If then in the church one goes hungry
while another has more than needed,
the reality of the church is violated.

Samuel Rayan, India, adapted

You are invited to eat this simple breakfast as an act of solidarity with those for whom a single piece of bread must suffice for today, as well as a reminder of the millions who cannot be confident of any food.

Index of Music

Agios o Theos 42
Alegria 103
Aleluia (Brazil) 85
Alleluja (Russia) 138
Amen 165
An den Wassern 105
As many as have been baptized 100
Bleibet hier 59
By the waters 105
Chantez la joie 103
Christ, soleil resplendissant 95
Chuyo chuyo 159
Ch'iu Chu 73
Come, O Holy Spirit come 54
Come Holy Spirit 148
Come to be our hope, O Jesus 160
Come down, O Love divine 137
Där Guds Ande är 125
De aarde is vervuld 35
Dein Will' gescheh', o Herr 32
Der, voghormia 109
Dieu saint, Dieu saint, Dieu saint 37
Dieu saint, Dieu saint, Dieu saint 142
Dieu aie pitié 86
Dios, danos fuerza 130
Dios hizo al agua cristalina 117
Du är helig 112
Du bist heilig 112
Du Lebensgrund 116
Ehre, Ehre, Ehre 121
El cielo canta alegría 28
En ce temps aujourd'hui 134
En tiempo como este 134
Enviado soy de Dios 52
Envíame Dios 150
Envoyé par Dieu 52
Eres santo 112
Espíritu de Dios, ven 131
Esprit de Dieu, descends 131
For such a time as this 134
For the fruit of all creation 62
From all that dwell below the
    skies 141
Giver of life 116
Gloire, gloire, gloire 121
Gloire soit à Dieu 72

Gloria a Dios 31
Gloria, gloria, gloria 121
Glory to God 31
God made the crystal clear waters 117
God of all the world 84
Gospodi pomiluj 63
Gud skapade de klara vattnen 117
Hágase tu voluntad 32
Halle-Halle-Halleluja 76
Halleluia (Indonesia) 114
Hallelujah (Zimbabwe) 61
Hallelujah (Ghana) 129
Have mercy on us, Lord 145
Heaven is singing for joy 28
Heilig, heilig, heilig, heilig 65
Heilig, heilig, heilig 37
Heilig, heilig, heilig ist Gott 142
Heiliger Geist, komm 148
Holy, holy, holy Lord of power 142
Holy, holy, holy 37
Holy, holy, holy, holy 65
I am the vine 50
I will sing to the Lord 158
Imegmoy pitak ay yay 41
In einer Zeit wie jetzt 134
Je veux chanter au Seigneur 158
Jesu tawapano 58
Jesus Christ, Son of God 57
Jesus, radiant sun so bright 95
Jeya ho 97
Joyfully sing 103
Junto a los ríos 105
Khudaya, rahem kar 145
Komm, Gottes Geist, komm herab 131
Komm, o komm Heiliger Geist 54
Kuda Kwenyu 67
Kyrie eleison (Armenia) 109
Kyrie eleison (Ukraine) 31
Kyrie eleison (Ghana) 51
Kyrie eleison (Greece) 92
Là où est l'Esprit 125
Lågorna ärmånga 78
Laudate omnes gentes 93
L'eau viv', et la pluie sur les champs 117
Let my prayer rise before you 145
Look, the Lamb of God 106

Lord have mercy 86
Lord, have mercy on us 73
Lord, your hands have formed this world 41
Louons le Créateur 155
Many and great 48
Many are the lightbeams 78
Masithi 75
Merci à Toi Seigneur 123
Mi pela i bung 84
Muchas y grandes 48
Muchos resplandores 78
Munezero 103
Nada te turbe 139
Nkosi, Nkosi 86
Nothing can trouble 139
Now thank we all our God 155
Nun danket alle Gott 155
Nyame Ne Sunsum, Sian Brao 131
O Dieu de vie 116
O God give us power 130
O Gott gib uns Stärke 130
O healing river 91
O, Lamb of God 166
O Seigneur, donne-nous ta puissance 130
O viens, Esprit, viens 54
Oh, freedom 127
Oh, Lord, have mercy on us 107
Oh Creador 116
Oi, Jumalan Karitsa 166
Our Father, which art in heaven 101
Pour rendre grâce à Dieu 35
Praise with joy the world's Creator 72
Prends-moi Seigneur 150
Puji Tuhan 114
Que ta volonté soit faite 32
Quiconque est baptisé 100
Quien fue bautizado 100
Reamo leboga 123
Regardez, l'agneau de Dieu 106
Santo, santo, santo 37
Santo, santo, santo, santo 65
Santo, santo, santo y poderoso
   Dios 142
Seigneur, aie pitié de nous 107
Sele 140
Send me Lord 150

Sende mich Herr 150
Senhor, tempiedade de nós 107
Señor, ten piedad de nosotros 107
Sent by the Lord am I 52
Shalom sawidi a paz 166
Siehe, das ist Gottes Lamm 106
Sing amen 75
Singt Amen 75
Siph' amandla Nkosi 130
Siyahamb' 45
Sonne der Gerechtigkeit 95
Stay with me 59
Strahlen brechen viele 78
Sur les rives 105
Ten piedad Señor 86
The Lord is my light 43
The whole earth is fulfilled 35
Those who wait on the Lord 55
Thuma mina 150
Tous ensemble 84
Très saint, très saint, très saint, très
   saint 65
Tu es saint 112
Tú Jesús, nuestra esperanza 160
Ubi caritas 81
Unless a grain of wheat shall fall 39
Vem, Jesus nossa esperança 160
Ven Espíritu Santo 148
Veni Sancte Spiritus 164
Viens Jésus notre espérance 160
Viens, Esprit Saint 148
Wa Wa Wa Emimimo 54
We are marching in the light of God 45
We give our thanks to Him 123
We believe: Maranatha 60
We're going to shine like the sun 68
When you, O Lord 89
Where the Spirit is 125
Wieviele von euch getauft 100
Wir danken unserm Gott 123
Wir versammeln uns 84
Wo der Geist wohnt 125
You are holy 112
You shall go out with joy 33
Your will be done 67
Your will be done, O Lord 32
Zahlreich und groß 48

Sources

We wish to thank all those who have granted permission for the use of prayers, hymns and liturgical responses in this book. We have made every effort to trace and identify them correctly and to secure all the necessary permissions for reprinting. If we have erred in any way in the acknowledgments, or have unwittingly infringed any copyright, we apologize sincerely.

The acknowledgments for music occur at the end of each piece.

For the prayers we have used the following sources:

© *Dorothy McRae-McMahon, P.O. Box 1724, Rozelle NSW 2039, Australia*

p. 115	"O God, into the pain of the tortured"
pp. 140-141	"In mystery and grandeur"
pp. 148-149	"Come, Holy Spirit, Renew the Whole Creation"

© *Wild Goose Resource Group, The Iona Community, Pearce Institute, Govan, Glasgow G51 3UU, United Kingdom*

p. 30	"Before the world existed"
pp. 30-31	"Let us pray with Abraham and Sarah"
pp. 32-33	"We bring to you the wastelands of the earth, O God"
p. 33	"May the love of God enfold us"
p. 35	"From before the world began"
pp. 36-37	"Remember not the former things"
pp. 40-41	"In the beginning"
p. 42	"Jesus said: I am the light of the world"
pp. 42-43	"Maker of Light and lover of humankind"
	(The section "O God, you have opened to us the sea of your mercy... [until] and bind us close to you and to each other" adapted from a prayer from Syria)
pp. 56-57	"Lord, your ways are not our ways"
	(The section "Lord, in these times... [until] We ask this in Jesus' name" adapted from a prayer from the Philippines)
pp. 58-59	"Let us join in a litany of waiting"
pp. 60-62	"Out of chaos, you created order"
p. 70	"The world belongs to God"
pp. 71-72	"Glory to you, Almighty God"
pp. 73-75	"If we have worshipped you as a relic from the past"
p. 77	"Out of the depths we cry to you, O Lord"
pp. 116-117	"Glory to you, Almighty God"
pp. 145-146	"If we have been singing praises with our voices"

Prayers and poems from other sources:

p. 95	"Almighty God, gracious Lord"
	Prayer reprinted from the Lutheran Book of Worship, © 1978, by permission of Augsburg Fortress, USA.

pp. 121-122	"O God, the source of our being" In *All Desires Known*, by Janet Morley, published by SPCK, London, © Janet Morley 1992.
pp. 171-172	"If the Lord's disciples keep silence..." © Kathy Galloway, 20 Hamilton Park Ave, Glasgow G12 8DU, Scotland.
p. 174	"I am no longer afraid of death..." © Julia Esquivel, 20 Avenida 3-61, Zona 11, Colonia Mirador I, Ciudad de Guatemala, Guatemala.
p. 179	"Shared bread is the experience of people as community..." © Samuel Rayan, 23 Raj Niwas Marg, New Delhi 110 054, India.

Ateliers et Presses de Taizé
p. 43	"The Lord is my light"
p. 59	«Stay with Me»
p. 81	"Ubi Caritas"
p. 93	"Laudate Omnes Gentes"
p. 159	"Chuyo chuyo"
p. 164	"Veni Sancte Spiritus"
p. 139	"Nada Te Turbe"

Centre national de pastorale liturgique
| p. 35 | "Pour rendre grâce à Dieu" |

CopyCare Ltd
| p. 33 | "You shall go out with joy" |

CopyCare Deutschland
p. 39	"Unless a grain of wheat"
p. 97	"Jeya ho"
p. 127	"Oh, freedom!" (arrangement)

Oxford University Press
| p. 137 | "Come Down O Love Divine" |
| p. 141 | "From all that dwell" (arrangement) |

Matti Rantatalo
| p. 166 | "Oi, Jumalan" |

Stainer & Bell, Ltd
| p. 35 | "The whole earth is fulfilled" |
| p. 62 | "For the fruit of all Creation" |

Olle Widestrand
| p. 78 | "Lågorna är många" |